Off The Porch

By Dick Jones

**First Edition
First Printing**

Off The Porch

Copyright 2012 by Dick Jones

Published by:

Dick Jones

USA

All rights reserved no portion of this book may be reproduced in any form, stored in retrieval system or transmitted in any form or by any means - electronic, mechanical, photocopy, recording, or any other - except brief quotations in printed reviews, without the prior written permission from author.

ISBN-10: 1495454657
ISBN-13: 978-1495454653
Library of Congress Catalog Number

Table of Contents

Benefits of Dove Hunting in the South 1
Appreciation of the Raw Oyster. 9
Big Pete in the Darkness. 17
Bobby Learns to Read 23
Bernie and the New York Deer Hunt 31
Dr. Dick and the Auction. 37
Duck Fever 43
Bill and the Christmas Puppy 49
Dr. Dick's New Truck. 55
Jake and the Dove Spot .61
Christmas Duck Hunt. 67
Doc and the Big School of Drum. 75
Everything Grows Fast in Summer 81
I Learn About Insect Control. 87
Evander's Deer Club Goes to Work for Big Bucks 93
The Value of Optimism. 99
Merwin and Evander and the Bird Dogs Grave . .105
Miz Liza and Jimmy Beane. 111
Nothing Like a Sure Thing. 115
On Choosing Summer Attire 125
One Turkey is as Good as Another 131
Russell Jones and the UFO Sighting 139
Say the Blessing, Bob 145
Sometimes It's Better to be Wrong 151
Striper Run for Stumpy .157
Texas Trickery. 167
The Lie as Art. 173
The Value of Time 179

Vinny and Roxanne and the Two Way Radios .. 185
White Ford Lies........................ 191
William Angel......................... 197
Dave and Toots and the Ivory Box.......... 203
Eddy, Evander and the Big Fish 213
Why Uncle Evander Left New Orleans....... 225
Bob and the White 40 Quart Cooler........ 239
Uncle Evander Steals a Watermelon......... 245

Book Intro

I know we're all wired differently. What inspires one goes totally unnoticed by another. There's one natural occurrence that happens twice every day, and it always resets my mind and puts me in a peaceful state of gratitude. I feel the same every time I experience it. From first contact with the horizon until breaking away, a sunset or sunrise lasts about three minutes. Those three minutes are the most inspiring time of my life, whether they hearken the dawn of a new day or signal the beginning of a new night.

I've experienced it from a duck blind and from a deer stand. Many times, I've witnessed it standing in surf and sand on the beach with a surf rod or walking across a rifle range and even on the road while traveling, but the effect is always the same. I watch, and think during this short three minute segment of my life. It's a time to be grateful for another day lived, or another night of rest. One can only enjoy a sunrise or sunset when outside, and outside is where I've found the most peace in my life.

Even though God's natural creation is inspiring, no human soul grows and develops independent of those around him. Every experience we live changes us forever in some way. Some changes are for good and develop character and benevolence in us. Others create weakness and inhibition. I was blessed to be born a son of the gentle South with loving parents who loved each other as much as they loved their family.

I grew up surrounded by good men and women

of character who set an example for me. My role models had a love of the outdoors, whether fishing, hunting, or working. The best days of my youth were spent outdoors and every sunrise or sunset always takes me back to those days and those people and it inspires me to be a better person.

The characters in this book are real. Some bear their own names, others not. Most stories involve humor and all reflect actual things that happened. Every situation in my life has been aided by the ability to find humor in it. Both good circumstances and bad ones are improved by the ability to make light of the situation. It's my wish that those who read this book will get a laugh. I also hope what you read in these pages makes you appreciate the outdoors and inspires you to love your fellow man a little more. God created all of us with flaws and all of us with charms.

I've stolen every story and character in this book from those people who've lived their lives in my presence. Some are close friends, others I wouldn't know if they walked up to me on the street. I want to thank the ones who've been closest to me for their support, love, and friendship. For those I casually encountered, I thank them for being who they are in making themselves memorable. For those I know well, I want to thank you for your influence in making my life richer. I also want to thank those who wrote the books I've enjoyed for teaching me the pleasure of reading what an imaginative mind can create. For those who taught and inspired me, thank you, especially my friend and neighbor, Mrs. Elizabeth Hayworth, who, a very long time ago, read something I wrote and thought it funny and worth looking at twice. I especially want to thank Cherie, my wife, for the best fifteen years of my life.

For the most part, I've lived my life outside the urban world where people live in close proximity yet they fear conversation with each other. I despise the mindset of not talking to strangers. My practice is to talk to everyone I come in contact with. I think every person God made has something of value to share. I love small towns and remote areas in the South where you can have a half hour conversation with a total stranger. I have a lot to be grateful for but the most important is that I was born who I am and where I am, here in rural North Carolina, surrounded by wonderful people.

Benefits of Dove Hunting in the South

There are people who don't understand a dove hunt. They say it doesn't have anything to do with hunting and I tend to agree with them on that point. My Uncle Evander Pritchart never called it a dove hunt; he called it a dove shoot and he saw it as a southern redneck kind of driven game shoot. It was not legal to bait doves, but the way Uncle Evander did it, the result was the same. There was always a large field planted to be harvested around Labor Day or a field of something planted to replenish the soil that just happened to be bush hogged around the time for the season to start. Oftentimes, it wouldn't be convenient to bush hog the field all in one day and it would get a few passes every week for a month or so. This had the "incidental" effect of providing forage at the same field for a long enough time that every dove in the county located it and came there for breakfast and dinner.

    The first day of the season and Labor Day were really special occasions with lots of friends and relatives of friends showing up with an eccentric collection of dogs, guns, and styles of dress.

There would be everything from Purdeys and Perrazis, to Stevens single barrels and Mossberg 500s. Most of those years, I shot a twenty gauge Winchester 101 and Uncle Evander carried his 16 gauge Fox. I wondered at the time why he would use such an ancient old thing when he could have afforded the best over-under money could buy. In later years, when the shooting was slow, I sat on a dove bucket with that same old Fox across my knees and thought of how thickheaded I was as a youth for thinking that. It is my favorite dove gun now, slim and six pounds, choked light modified and improved modified; it is a pleasure to carry and shoot.

We normally socialized for hours before the shooting began. There were hot dogs and hamburgers for lunch and plans would be made for supper. Most birds don't fly until the shadows start getting a little longer and the old seasoned shooters just smoked cigars, talked shotguns, and gossiped until that time. The action would really heat up at about four in the afternoon. I was young, but I learned fast about going out early. The first couple of hunts with my uncle, I was first in the field thinking that these old guys didn't care about hunting and only wanted to gossip. After swatting dog pecker gnats and sweating in the heat to pick up two birds and then having my uncle come off the field with his limit before me due to his superior shooting, I learned better. Besides, you could learn a lot listening to the gossip and shotgun talk.

The first two days of dove hunting, the Saturday before Labor Day and Labor Day itself were always accompanied with some sort of feast.

These were high holy days for my uncle and his friends because they marked the beginning of the gunning season. There would be watermelons or sometimes cider for refreshment. Perhaps someone would drive over to the local barbeque place for food, but more likely, there would be a fish fry of recently caught catfish, or we would wrap the dove breasts in bacon and cook them on the grill on the edge of the field. One of my favorite dove shoot dinners was when Uncle Evander had us clean the breasts and filet them off the bone. He would then fry the tiny filets in olive oil and House Autry Seafood Breader and make gravy. Kind of a chicken fried dove. He'd make mashed potatoes, cook some carrots with lots of pepper and butter, and make a huge pan full of cat-head biscuits. Somehow, he could accomplish this in about thirty minutes. There was barely enough time to recap all the funny shots and dog blunders before food was on the table.

One of my favorite places to hunt was in Tyrrell County. I (and everybody else for that matter) pronounced it different from Uncle Evander but he seemed not to notice. He had this thing about pronouncing something the way the man it was named for would have said it; he said it was out of respect; most people assumed he just wanted to be different.

The field I'm thinking of was right alongside Highway 64 not far from the Alligator River, on the way to Whalebone Junction and Cape Hatteras. I still pass it every time I go down there, and it kind of twists my heart a little every time I come around the gentle bend in the road and see it. There was a little house along the road that was actually in the field and nobody lived in it. Bob Craft's family owned it and he cleaned it out each year before the hunting season to use as a camp. Uncle Evander had a big trunk that he filled with his cooking stuff, and he stocked the kitchen just before dove season and cleaned it out at the end of the last duck season. We slept in it, but most of the other guys we hunted with down there were locals and slept in their own beds. It had a wood stove, but we used the old white gas range to heat it in all but the coldest duck trips. It may have had paint on it at one time, but I never saw any evidence of it. The tin roof was solid rust, and it may leak now, but it never did when I was sleeping in it. There were two bedrooms with two single beds in each, but Evander and I always slept in the same room whether we had company or not. There was a large table with chairs that didn't match in the kitchen and a sitting room with a dusty old couch. It still stands, surrounded by scrubby trees so thick that it looks like a thicket for three seasons of the year. I can only see the windows and doors now when I go past it on late season trips for stripers.

    At my uncle's shoots, we only shot a limit. We didn't partake in the excess that sometimes finds its way into Southern dove hunts. Uncle Evander more than once explained to me that giving in to excess is what separates men of character from greedy slobs. Years later, at a hunt in Roberson County where I exceeded my limit exponentially, I thought about what he'd said. There was no more fun in killing a big pile of birds, than in getting a limit and taking a slow walk back to the truck with what the law said was a reasonable take. I don't exceed my limit anymore, and I can't even get worked up about the hunts in exotic places where you can kill hundreds of birds. I think I'd just feel guilty.

Late dove season was even better than early since it wasn't so hot and was blended in with duck hunting and fishing trips. On trips there in the late fall, my mother required two things to be brought in as booty in exchange for Uncle Evander borrowing me for a hunting/fishing trip. One item was a bushel of sweet potatoes for baking that was sold under a couple of slabs of tin roof beside of NC 64 on the honor system. The other was a peck bucket full of pecans. Across the road from the old house, there was a large grove of pecan trees and, at some point during the trip, I'd go over there and pick up a bucketful. I always hated picking stuff in the garden, but this was different. It was always late fall and there were leaves on the ground. Sometimes, as I remember, I did it after a mourning dove hunt, and then putting the little Carolina boat in the Alligator River and catching a few schoolie size stripers.

It wasn't hard to muster up the resolve to complete the task because it was so pleasant and quiet in the pecan grove. Far enough off the road that you just barely could hear the cars, there was a thicket of over grown boxwoods and a chimney where an old plantation house had stood with a five acre pond just beyond that. It was also easier because I knew that the nuts would wind up in Mom's fruit cakes and become pecan pies come Christmas.

One year, there was an Indian summer. It was into the wood duck season as we called it, and it was warm as late August in the days, though cool at night. One really nice afternoon after a morning duck hunt, I told Uncle Evander that I was going to gather the pecans. He said that he'd go with me, and we'd see if any ducks were using the pond behind the pecan orchard. The pond back there looked like a picture over somebody's couch when the leaves were changing. It had cattails on one end and it was surrounded with grass and live oaks.

After we got our peck of pecans and started down the trail to the pond, we noticed a little red Dodge Dart convertible parked in the field where the box bushes were. While it didn't look like a car one of the local guys who fished the pond drove, I assumed someone was fishing since we couldn't see it from the pecan grove.

As we got close, we heard laughter and feminine voices. We came around the old bushes and saw that they were strewn with female clothing and underwear. There were four college age girls in the pond, and it was obvious from their clothes in the bushes, they were skinny dipping.

My blood pressure and pulse, as a pre-drivers-license teenage boy, probably went off the charts. On seeing us, they became quiet and moved to the far side of the pond. A blonde girl eyed us with more suspicion than fear and then spoke up. "We're not coming out of the water until after you leave," she said with surprising boldness.

Uncle Evander looked at me, held up the bucket, and grinned, "I didn't come here to run you off; ya'll can swim as long as you like; we just came here to feed the alligator.

Appreciation of the Raw Oyster

My uncle couldn't stand the idea of wasting time. He had this sense of life being such a precious thing that it was sinful not to use every minute to the fullest. He wanted to wring every moment out of every day and savor each experience. It wasn't that he couldn't sit and talk and waste time; he could spend hours just sitting in a lawn chair talking to someone he found interesting or someone that he felt needed to talk to someone. Often, however, he would take such people fishing, or help them do something trivial that allowed conversation while accomplishing something worthwhile, like fishing or duck hunting.

Like all teenagers, I had social problems, and he was a master at putting them into perspective. Sometimes, he would bring eight or ten of his fishing reels and a box filled with line, and we'd re-spool my reels and his while we talked. It took me years to figure out that these spooling sessions were his way of helping me at the same time he did something that needed to be done anyway. Not only did I have nice new line on my reels, I had a better perspective on life and how things that are important now, might not be so important later.

Every year, my family went to the beach for a week, and Evander often visited us while we were there. I, being the only boy on the trip, got to room with the energetic bachelor. It was also his pleasure to immerse me in his style of intense fishing. I was young and he was old, but I still couldn't hang with him when it came to fishing. He had this thing about seeing the sun rise and set every day that he could, and that meant that on his trips he was up before the sun every day. He had a way of making the prospects of the next day so promising that he could manage to get a teenage boy up at 5:00 a.m. We'd slip out of the rented beach cottage in total darkness. If we could see a strip of light on the horizon, he'd rush to get out on the hole he had picked out so he could be standing in the edge of the surf with a rod in his hand when the first rays of light came over the horizon. He didn't like to talk while the sun was on the horizon. That two or three minutes he reserved for his own thoughts, and it didn't take me long to figure out, he didn't want to talk then. I decided it was a nice habit, and I still do that very thing.

We'd fish till nine or so, more if the tide was close to high, and then we'd eat breakfast. If we had fish to clean, he'd clean them and keep me busy on trivial chores to keep me from asking to help. He secretly loved to clean fish, though he acted like it was a task he did out of consideration for others. He told me once that cleaning fish well, or sweeping the floor well, for that matter, was just as important as playing the violin well. There is art in everything we do, and there can be as much satisfaction in a well-cleaned fish as in a well-painted picture.

Appreciation of the Raw Oyster

After the fish were cleaned, bagged, and in the freezer or on ice, he'd offer me a nap, citing how early I'd gotten up. I never took this offer because I knew the next part of the day could easily be the best. Normally, it didn't directly involve fishing. Sometimes he'd get word, or perhaps he just had a hunch, and we'd go to some spot on the sound or the inlet for a fishing foray, but, normally, we'd attend to some detail that was necessary for the business of fun he was engaged in. Our middle of the day trips included: scouting places to duck hunt during late season, driving inland fifty or so miles to talk to a landowner about a bird or dove hunting spot, visiting one of his endless list of friends for the purpose of showing off or trading a shotgun or just to check up on them and sit on their porch and drink ice tea.

One of the most fun trips was going out in the marsh to get oysters. My parents weren't the raw oyster type. They preferred their oysters in a stew. Not a bad soup, but the boiled oysters tasted to me like pencil erasers. Evander would eat oyster stew with the family, but he probably wouldn't have done it in public. He was a purist when it came to oysters and he liked them raw. He knew where to find them, probably tipped off by his salty beach friends, and I thought it to be high adventure. We'd gather a bushel or so and sit in the boat while he produced Texas Pete sauce and Zesta saltine crackers (no other brand would do), and thus, was I introduced to the very adult practice of eating raw oysters. He always had a cooler of little 6 oz. Cokes and sometimes a more adult beverage for himself. I can still taste the salty, coppery taste of the oyster with the sweet/hot Texas Pete and the salty-crisp cracker followed with the fizzy electric taste of those little Cokes. I still keep them in the old Kelvinator refrigerator on my front porch. That refrigerator is as old or older than I am, and I know full well it'll outlast the one we bought five years ago.

To get back to the raw oyster eating education, though, I have to say it was invaluable.

A little later in life, I got a chance to go to a nice restaurant with my friends. I ordered raw oysters. Battle scars from World War II could not have made me more of a man of the world as eating those oysters. The funny thing is that they were terrible in comparison to the oysters I learned to appreciate through Evander's treachery. I ate them with gusto, though, and I made a point to mention that they were a little small.

The excellence of the first ones I ate in the marsh was the product of devious planning on the part of my illustrious uncle. He knew full well that I'd have never eaten a raw oyster unless I was starving. On the day of my introduction, after our morning fishing, he took me to breakfast at a place known for waffles, and we had waffles. Waffles do not stick with me, and he knew this. We then launched his little Carolina boat and headed up the Intercoastal Waterway with a cooler of ice and his homemade version of a live well. Our objective was to scout a potential duck hunting spot he had heard of, catch some peanut mullet for Sam Blake to flounder fish with, and get some oysters for Sam and Grandma. Grandma was not any one's grandmother, not that she wouldn't have made a terrific grandma. Sam's wife was lovingly called Grandma by most of the people who knew her because of her long grey hair and wire rim glasses.

Appreciation of the Raw Oyster

We were also going to get some oysters for Mom to make a stew for supper. We were on the water by ten thirty, and it was after noon before we finished scoping out the duck hole. The weather was a perfect October day: cool enough to need a jacket when the boat was running, but warm enough to sweat if you were working. Evander found a school of mullet, and, with a couple of casts of his big cast net, we had more than the little bait system could keep alive, so we culled them to fit Sam's size preferences and tossed back the rest. Next came the oysters. By this time, I was starving. I suggested we eat. Evander always had food on the boat, and I had a pilgrim's faith that today was no different.

Evander was evasive and suggested we gather the oysters first. When we had a bushel on ice (this didn't really take all that long), he opened the little door under the bow sheets where he kept the snacks. The little Playmate cooler contained nothing but drinks: no cheese and no sandwiches. The knapsack contained only Zesta saltines and Texas Pete. I ate a couple of crackers plain and dry and then was seduced by the way the oysters looked when Evander ate them. The first one was a little scary but by the third, I was a raw oyster eater for life. If there had been one pack of Nabs (Southern for cheese crackers) in that knapsack, my life might have been different. I believe their absence was intentional, as it was the only time I can remember when Evander was short of this staple of life.

I got back to the boat dock feeling like more of a man than when the little voyage had begun, but there was no time for reflection. We delivered the mullet and oysters to Sam and Grandma, picked up some pogies for bait for the evening's fishing

Appreciation of the Raw Oyster

session, shucked the rest of the oysters for Mom's stew, and headed for the little hole below the rocks at Fort Fisher for the evening bite.

When the time came, Evander turned to watch the sun go down over the dunes and we fished on till after high tide. We caught a couple of nice puppies, a big sea trout after it got dark, and the little blues quit stealing our bait. Evander took the time to explain to me how to tell by the moon when high tide was. I still use the method of extending my arm and gauging the moon's height over the horizon at the distance occupied from the tip of my extended thumb to the extended tip of my little finger. It's pretty accurate, and if I can see the moon, I can pretty well tell you what the tide is. However, I cannot do it without thinking of this old man who had the patience to spend his whole day with an insecure fourteen-year-old boy with acne.

Appreciation of the Raw Oyster

We quit fishing at about nine thirty and by ten thirty the fish were in the little freezer of the Kelvinator that looked just like the one that is now on my front porch. Evander heated up some of Mom's oyster stew and, as I ate it, I knew that I would never again eat it without thinking that it was a waste of perfectly good oysters.

As I climbed up into the upper bunk, Evander asked me if I wanted him to get me up when he got up. "I got a feelin' that the Spanish mackerel will hit Gotcha plugs off the Steel Pier just about sun-up," he said, lying on his back with his arms behind his head. I told him to call me when he got up and we'd give it a try.

Big Pete in the Darkness

My Uncle Evander had a disdain for flashlights. Not to say he didn't believe in them; in fact, he had one of the nicest flashlights I ever saw. It was a little AA battery job that he wore on a lanyard around his neck. He only used it when he really needed it. He got aggravated with people who were addicted to light. He would grumble to me about how some folks kept their light on all the time and blinded him with it when, if they would have turned it off and let their eyes adjust, they could have seen a lot better.

Evander was not adverse to dabbling in all kinds of outdoor activities, so when he called me one Thursday to ask if I wanted to try coon hunting, I wasn't surprised. In fact, I was delighted. The idea of traipsing around in the woods at night listening to dogs sounded like the kind of adventure a pre-drivers-license Ledford boy would go for.

For those who've never tried coon hunting, you should try it. It's a very different type of hunting; everything is about the dogs and the sounds they make. On a good coon hunt, the dogs are released and the hunters listen and wait. It's a great time to smoke a cigar or enjoy the night sounds. There are a lot of low conversations since everyone is listening for the baying of the dogs.

Once the dogs strike on a trail, there are conversations about where they're going and how to intercept. Of course, the action picks up once the dogs tree. The hunters can instantly tell if the coon's gone up a tree, and suddenly the hunters burst into action. The best route to the dogs is determined and it's never easy. There are all kinds of end strategies for a coon hunt: from shooting the coon out of the tree to simply leashing the dogs and leaving. It's not about the finish; it's about the race.

The deal was that Evander, Charlie Saintsing, and Al Collins were going to Bud Sinks place and run the coons. I was thrilled to go, but I had some reservations about spending a lot of time with Al. Al was a big man who tended to be loud and bragged a lot about his dogs, his truck, his guns, and everything else he had. He also treated me as persona non grata, since he seemed to see me as a wet nosed kid. In fact, I was a wet nosed kid but most of Evander's friends had the ability to make me feel like an equal. I never did understand why Evander invited Al to come on excursions, but I figured out as I grew older that the old man felt a little sorry for him.

My first night of coon hunting was fairly uneventful: we managed to tree a coon, Charlie's dogs did great, Al's dogs seemed to not quite have the hang of it, and Al continually bragged on them anyway. One dog, Boomer, was particularly obnoxious. Al kept him on a leash most of the time because he was hard to catch, and he constantly kept Al off balance by surging on the leash. Al seemed

Big Pete in the Darkness

not to notice and bragged on him anyway. Al had a habit of saying something and looking you right in the face, blinding you with the lamp he had strapped on his head. He never turned it off even though it was a moonlit night, and once your eyes adjusted, you could see your own shadow.

Late in the night, we stopped on the top of a bluff on Jimmy Sinks farm. We were standing around listening to the dogs when Evander let out a low moan like a softly bellowing heifer. A few minutes later, we heard a crashing in the woods. Something was crashing around in the thicket at the bottom of the bluff, and it was big. It was Al who spoke up first, "What the heck is that?" He kept his head lamp pointed in the direction of the sound.

I imagined a bull elephant or perhaps a rhino or Cape buffalo. A small sapling tall enough to reach almost to the top of the bluff began to shake. Evander chuckled, "That's just old Pete."

"Who is Pete?" Al gasped.

Evander chuckled again. "Pete's Bud's prize Holstein bull. He's the meanest bull I ever saw, but don't worry; there's a fence between us. Pete is so mean that Bud has to drive the tractor into the pasture to get around. Pete pushes against the tractor wheels and bellows the whole time. One time, Pete broke the injector pump off the tractor, and Bud had to wait for Jimmy to come and get him on his tractor and tow him in. Pete's so mean he would give Juan Belmonte, the famous bull fighter, a hard time."

Al insisted on taking the path down to the fence line to see Pete. Pete was as ferocious as any bovine I ever saw, standing in the edge of the thicket with steam blowing from his nostrils and his eyes glowing red in the reflection of Al's flashlight. Al was like a kid at a haunted house, fascinated, but scared to death. "That bull gives me the willies," he mumbled as we climbed back up the bluff.

Two weeks later, we went again with the same group. This time, Al and Boomer seemed to get on even Evander's nerves. Boomer surging against the leash, Al bragging and flashing his head light in everyone's eyes, and swearing at Boomer while he told us how much potential the dog had. At one point, the dogs treed about a half mile away. Boomer was still on the leash as we headed to the sound of the baying dogs. Al was blowing like a steam engine, his weight wearing him out, and fighting the surging Boomer aggravated the problem.

When we reached the fence, Evander slipped right under it and headed across the pasture. Al froze and called to Evander, "What about Pete?"

Evander stopped and paused a second, "Do you want to walk an extra half mile around the pasture?"

Al considered. "Let's walk fast," he said, and once he and Boomer were under the fence, they headed across the field in high speed, Boomer jerking Al along and the headlamp bouncing light on the ground just in front of them. Charlie, Evander, and I came along at a more leisurely pace.

We were about halfway across when Evander pulled up and stopped. I sensed trouble, and in a voice just loud enough for Al to hear, Evander said, "Evening, Pete."

Everyone froze in an instant. You could hear Al's breath heaving. The light raised up to reveal steaming nostrils and red eyes.

Al jerked Boomer's leash so hard the dog yelped, and the both of them raced back across the field at a speed I could not imagine Al's considerable bulk could have accomplished.

We stood silently. The black and white form hovered in the darkness just a few yards away. "What should we do?" I asked.

"Running from a bull is the worst thing you can do," Charlie said with little concern.

Evander seemed unnaturally relaxed in the face of danger. I trusted the two men and never moved.

"Well, there's three of us, if we split up, two of us are sure to be OK," Evander said, still calm. "In fact, I'm pretty sure that all three of us are going to be OK."

"How can you say that?" I stammered. "You don't seem to be worried at all." The steaming form was silent just a few yards away.

Evander chuckled, "Well, the main reason I'm so calm is that that's not Pete. We're not in Pete's pasture; we're in Bossy's pasture, and Bossy is Bud's old milk cow. Boy, that Al can really move when he wants to, huh? Ya'll want to call him back now before he gets out of the county?"

Bobby Learns to Read

In his youth, Bobby Robichaux was one of the best duck guides in the St. Bernard Parish. He was tall with short cropped hair and a perpetual smile. Bobby was proud of his Cajun heritage and his ability to find ducks. Not only could he find them, he could call them as well. Uncle Evander hunted with him a lot, and they were close friends. Bobby had a pretty normal life by most standards. He had a pretty wife and two cute little girls; he was a carpenter by trade and a good one; he drove an old beat-up pickup, but he had nice shotguns. Bobby couldn't read. He could figure all the things he needed to build a house, he was a great mechanic, he could reload his own shotgun shells, but he couldn't read.

On the other hand, my uncle was a prolific reader. He read everything from The Conquest of the Aztecs and Peru by Prescot one week and Zen and the Art of Motorcycle Maintenance the next. He read biographies, novels, and histories of all sorts. He liked books about scientific expeditions, philosophy, politics, and travel. He didn't read pulp as he called it. He didn't read detective stories, western novels

Bobby Learns to Read

(except maybe <u>Roping Lions in the Grand Canyon</u> by Zane Grey). He didn't read mysteries or science fiction or detective novels.

Evander told me once, life is too short to have time to do everything, so reading books helps you decide what to invest your time in next. "What you do in life is determined by your dreams," he said once, as we floated down a river watching our catfish jugs. "You can't decide you want to be an archaeologist if you don't know what one is." (At the time that was what I wanted to be because he had given me a book on dinosaurs.)

He went through his life collecting skills like a Boy Scout getting merit badges. Books helped him in his quest. He would pick up something new, read and learn all he could about it, work on it until he had achieved the desired level of success, and then donate enough time to it to maintain proficiency. He stayed busy in his later years maintaining some of his skills. He let some things slide of course. As he said, "Nobody wants to see a seventy year old man water ski." Even in his old age he still played harmonica well enough to sit in with a blues band if asked.

It was his philosophy that reading was a way to improve oneself. History, politics, and science made you more knowledgeable of the workings of the world. Philosophy and the Bible gave you insight into your fellow man, and how to live your life to the fullest. Technical reading helped you to flourish in life and accomplish your dreams. And literature, good literature, taught a person how to understand the inner workings of the human mind.

He kept ten books on a shelf that he said were the ten best books ever written. I won't bore you with the list, but he said that his life would not have been the same had he not read them. Most of them would have been classified in the literature category.

This story is about Bobby, however, and Evander told it like this:

He and Bobby had hunted together for several years in their youth, and Bobby and Evander had discussed Bobby's illiteracy. Bobby reasoned that he'd not really missed anything in life by not reading. Bobby couldn't read, but he'd established his own brand of philosophy, and he was a deep thinker. His point was that, since he didn't know what he was missing, his life was as fulfilled as that of any intellectual who'd ever lived. He reckoned there were things he could read that many other people couldn't, like the way mallard ducks moved their heads when they had decided to come in. Many less-schooled people would continue to call and perhaps spook the birds in doing so.

My uncle agreed with this, but still pressed for Bobby to learn to read, telling him it would make so many things in life easier. This argument had little effect on Bobby since, in his opinion, he had an easier and better life than almost everyone he knew. This was reinforced by the adoration of every doctor and lawyer that had ever hired Bobby to take them hunting. To a man, they had told him he had the perfect life.

Evander reminded Bobby of how people had told him the same thing. He told Bobby both of them had learned how to live in the world they had. They made it look easy and that was why people envied their lives. Bobby agreed in principle, but was unconvinced reading would improve him. Uncle Evander also suspected Bobby would never admit his life wasn't complete, since he had a competitive nature and was proud of his accomplishments. To have admitted that reading would improve his life now would mean that, at least until he learned to read, he wasn't a complete man. After a few such discussions, Evander didn't mention it further.

In the later years of their lives, Uncle Evander discovered striped bass. He'd known they existed; he just didn't know how much fun they were. By this time, his finances were solid enough to allow him to make forays to the places he had read and dreamed about. He went to Africa for a budget safari and visited an old rifle team member in Maine for some northern style hunting and fishing. He also took time to travel back to Louisiana for fishing and hunting with old friends.

When he discovered the spring striper run on the Roanoke River in his home state of North Carolina, it became a part of his spring routine.

He and Bobby had always hunted as friends, not as a client and guide, and they continued to do so. He always felt he owed Bobby for this hospitality, since he was hunting with a sought-after guide at no cost.

Bobby always took him to the very best spots because hunting with Evander was his fun hunting. Evander was always generous with his friends, and if he felt someone had been more generous than him, he tried to come up with a plan to set the table from the other side.

He came up with a plan to get on more even ground with Bobby by sending him a train ticket to Raleigh for the spring striper run on the Roanoke. Evander would pick Bobby up at the station, and they would stay at the Halifax Hotel, in Weldon, and fish out of his boat. The whole trip would be his treat.

Bobby was more than glad to go. He'd heard so many stories about striper fishing and, if it was half as good as Evander described it, it would be very good. Evander was a world-class liar and proud of it, but his references to good places to fish or hunt were always accurate. Some things are too important to lie about.

With one exception, the trip was perfect. The fish bit just as reported and Bobby, who'd fished all his life and lived in the middle of some of the best fishing in the country, told Evander on the first day that he had caught more fish than any other day in his life. Evander had the technique down pat. They'd drift down the river and catch fish on jigs or flies and then crank up and run back up for another drift. The hotel was simple, but nice, and the restaurants where they dined were cheap and good.

The waitress at the place where they ate breakfast treated them as if they were her grandfathers, making sure they had everything they needed and filling Bobby's Stanley thermos with good strong coffee for free. But it rained. It rained every day; not all day but every morning until about nine or ten. "Who cares if it's raining when you're catching fish?" they asked each other, and like always, they had fun in the weather they had.

One morning, Uncle Evander noticed something. Bobby bought a local paper and paid a nickel for it. He then realized that Bobby had bought one every morning of the trip. He chuckled to himself. Bobby, the scoundrel, had learned to read and had kept it a secret from him. Of course, he'd been responsible, since there'd been so many discussions about it. He was proud of how he'd influenced his old friend, and he even thought of what a great contribution he

Bobby Learns to Read

had made in Bobby's life. He laughed at himself for inviting Bobby on this trip so he could out-do him in generosity since he'd given Bobby, indirectly of course, one of the best gifts in life. All day, he wanted to question Bobby on it, but he knew that Bobby had chosen to hide his literacy for a reason, and he didn't want to push him. He decided to trick him into telling him. It appealed to him on another level, too. After all, it did involve tricking Bobby into the confession.

After supper that night, he worked out a plan to use in the morning. They'd been meeting in the restaurant every morning, and he got up early so he could beat Bobby there. He told Margret, the waitress, he'd give her a dollar tip if she could get Bobby to talk about reading. He suggested that she discuss things she'd read in the paper or books she'd read. He didn't tell her the whole story, just that it was a trick on Bobby, and she liked the idea.

When Bobby came to the table, Margret filled his coffee cup and asked Bobby if he'd read anything about the train wreck that had happened at Wilmington last week. Bobby said that he didn't trust trains and was nervous the whole trip up here, but he trusted airplanes even less. He ordered eggs and country ham.

When she brought his eggs and ham, she asked if he ever read his horoscope in the paper. Bobby answered that he'd like some orange juice. He said he'd forgotten to tell her and he was sorry she had to run back to the kitchen.

She looked at Evander and he figured she was thinking that this was some kind of setup, but she was determined. She left for the orange juice. When she brought the orange juice, she said that she was reading the most interesting book on striper fishing.

Bobby Learns to Read

This got Bobby's attention. "Is it about fishing around here?" he asked. She stumbled a little and said that it was about striper fishing everywhere. She looked at Evander for his reaction. His expression told her that this was not enough of a response to get the dollar.

Just at that time, the other waitress dropped a plate filled with food and the clatter could have been heard for a half-mile. Bobby looked around to see what happened, and the train of thought was lost. She looked exasperated and left the table.

When she came back to fill Bobby's thermos, she looked at Evander and then addressed Bobby. "What do you like to read, Mr. Bobby?" She was sure she had him this time.

"I never learned to read," he said, "and I've been so busy all my life that I never missed it." The triumphant smile left her young face, and she carried the thermos away to fill it.

"Bobby, you're a bigger liar than I am," Evander huffed. "I know you've learned to read because I've watched you buy a newspaper every morning."

"What has buying a newspaper got to do with reading?" Bobby asked.

Now it was Evander's turn to be exasperated. "Why else would you buy one? There aren't any pictures."

"I keep forgetting my hat and leaving it in the truck," Bobby said. "I use the newspaper to cover my head in the rain till I can get my hat out of your truck."

Evander groaned and laid a fresh new dollar on the table.

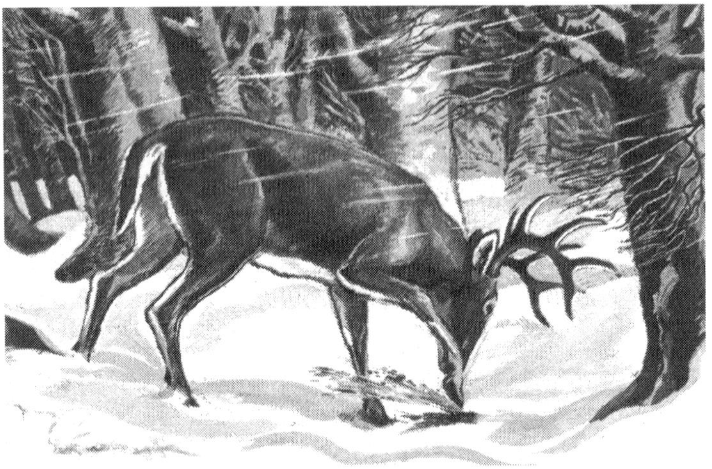

Bernie and the New York Deer Hunt

Later in life, Uncle Evander didn't deer hunt much, but he did enjoy it from time to time. The part he didn't like was sitting still while his feet turned to ice. He was cold natured, and I'd like to have a dollar for every time I heard him say under his breath, "Old man, cold man." He'd mutter it as we put out duck decoys, or when the north wind on Hatteras was particularly mean.

He did love to spend time with his brother in law, Bernie Tramacco, from Homer, New York. Bernie was a classic Italian-American. He didn't have an Italian accent because he was second generation, but he looked like he should have belonged to the Mafia and fell for Evander's pranks like a bluefish falls for a Hopkins. Evander got Bernie with countless phone pranks, rubber snakes, coon tails tied to door knobs, and every other practical joke you could think of. Bernie was Aunt Diane's favorite brother, and Evander told her once that if they got a divorce, he was keeping Bernie.

I was surprised when Evander told me he was going to New York for Thanksgiving to deer hunt, but I shouldn't have been because Evander was the most unpredictable man I ever knew. "Bernie says there's two big bucks that walk across the alfalfa field behind his house every morning and evening at the new house he's building. He'll be moved in by the time we get there, and I'll be able to just get up and walk to the stand and come in when I'm ready. Your aunt's been talking about that deer sausage we had the last time we were up there, and I haven't deer hunted in years."

I asked him about the issue of his feet getting cold. He muttered about some new boots he'd bought, and how it had been unseasonably warm this year. Then he went back to sorting through his dusty deer hunting gear.

By the time Evander and Diane got to Homer, the weather had turned cold, but there was no snow. Evander went into town, bought his hunting license, and then built a ladder stand out of leftover 2x4s from the new house. He put it in the woods next to the alfalfa field as Bernie instructed. Though Bernie had moved in, the house wasn't quite finished yet, and Bernie was working on it when Evander returned from placing the stand. "Where are you hunting in the morning?" Evander asked.

"I'm not going to hunt in the morning because I can't find my old license to get my new license. I'm sure I'll find it tomorrow when we unpack a few more boxes." Bernie seemed confident, but Evander felt sorry for him, since he knew Bernie was keener to hunt than he was.

Evander went to the stand early the next morning to give things time to settle down, and by the time shooting hours came, he wished he had waited at the house a little longer. He chided

Bernie and the New York Deer Hunt

himself for being soft and settled in to wait for the big buck with horns like a Cracker Barrel rocking chair on his head. He never came. The cold did come though, and it snuck in on Evander like an Indian with a scalping axe. First, his feet got cold; Evander had always had problems with cold feet, and his new miracle boots didn't keep them toasty as promised in the magazine ad. He resolved that he'd not dressed warmly enough and that his body was sacrificing the warmth of his feet to keep his organs warm. He had more clothes and figured he would just put on more this afternoon, that is, if he wasn't at the processors getting the big buck turned into Italian deer sausage.

By 9:00 a.m. Evander had all the fun he could take and came down off the stand. He walked along the little road that ran over the hill on the farm of Bernie's neighbor, Fred Forbes, looking for deer tracks. He wasn't disappointed when he didn't see them; the ground was frozen as hard as a rock. When he got back to the house, Bernie was still working on the house, trimming out windows in the back bedroom. Evander had coffee and helped him for the rest of the morning and into the afternoon. At 3:00 p.m. he decided it was time to go back out. This time, he put all his clothes on and though it was really cold with a whipping north wind, he stayed relatively comfortable until dark. Still no big deer, but it was a full moon, and he figured the deer were traveling later. He came into the house, had hot chocolate and helped Bernie with hanging a shower curtain rod until time to go to dinner.

As they drove to a restaurant to meet the girls (Evander was buying since he was enjoying Bernie's hospitality), he asked Bernie if they should stop at

Walmart to get his hunting license. "Christine looked in a dozen boxes and didn't find it. She's getting some more out of the garage tomorrow and I'm sure she'll find it then." Bernie still seemed upbeat, but Evander was sure he was disappointed and just putting a good face on it. He resolved to work on the house with him the next day instead of cruising the local gun shops looking for old Fox shotguns. Poor guy, he thought.

The next day was brutally cold, even for New York, and Evander could only stand to stay out there until about 8:30. By the time he came in, it was snowing and Bernie was sitting at the table finishing his coffee. "What do you plan to do today?" Evander asked, rubbing himself to warm up.

"I've got to get some shelves and rods in the closets so Christine can finish some unpacking. I'm sure she'll find my license today." Bernie was eternally optimistic. Evander thought about how Bernie's optimism might be what made him such an easy target for tricks. He felt a little bad about some of the pranks he'd played.

"I'll help," he volunteered, "it's too cold to be out in this weather anyway."

They got it all done and even found time to go out to Doug's Fish Fry for lunch. Evander picked up the tab though Bernie protested. Evander went to the stand about 3:30 and walked across the snow looking for tracks... nothing. It was cold, but he stayed comfortable enough. He decided not to hunt the next day and help Bernie put the tile down in the den and foyer. He wasn't seeing anything anyway, and it would be nice to sleep past 5:30. The next day, they all slept late and went out for breakfast at Frank and Mary's, a little diner in Cortland; they had hash and eggs, something Evander couldn't get in North Carolina.

As they were leaving, they met Pete Manns, Bernie's neighbor, who was telling about a big buck that one of his friends had gotten the day before. Evander asked Bernie if he thought it might be one of the deer he had been seeing, and he noticed that Pat gave Bernie a funny look. He figured that perhaps Yankees were somewhat possessive of their deer.

Evander and Diane were to leave on Sunday morning, and Christine cooked a big Italian dinner for them on Saturday night. "Well," Evander said expansively, sipping coffee in front of the coal stove, "At least we got the floor down. I just wish you could have found your old license so we could have hunted together."

Christine looked surprised, "Why would Bernie need his old license?"

Evander explained patiently that Bernie needed his old license to get his new license. Bernie didn't say anything.

"But he has his new license. Besides, we never see deer in that field. I don't know why you wanted to hunt there," she said just as patiently.

Evander was incredulous. "Bernie, why did you tell me there were deer when there weren't and that you wanted to hunt when you didn't?" Evander was getting really frustrated.

"Because I needed the help to get all this done, and I knew you wouldn't come up here and help me if I didn't."

Dr. Dick and the Auction

There are a lot of different kinds of addictions. Recently, I had a case of poison oak that reminded me of the nature of an addiction. The poison oak was on my hands, and under most circumstances, the itch was mild and didn't really bother me that much until one morning I began to rub my hands together. Although the itch wasn't that intense until I began to massage my fingers together; the pleasure of stimulating the itchy nerves was wonderful. The more I rubbed my fingers together, the better it felt. When I stopped, my fingers itched ten times as much as they had before I scratched them, and I had to rub them together again; the pleasure was intense, but I couldn't stop.

That's exactly the way it was with Dr. Dick White buying nice guns. Dr. Dick wasn't really a collector, he had every intention of using the guns he bought, it's just that there was no way he could ever have time to use them all. Dr. Dick loved all kinds of quality firearms, and he was knowledgeable about all kinds of quality guns. He loved fine Colt and Smith and Wesson pistols, and revolvers. He

Dr. Dick and the Auction

had a passion for pre '64 Winchesters, and he loved fine shotguns. He had a large basement vault that contained enough nice shotguns, rifles, and pistols to make a gun shop owner jealous. He just couldn't stop himself from buying a quality gun at a good price. The more he bought, the more he wanted to buy, and since he was more than adequately funded, he bought a lot of guns. It was just this addiction that inspired this story.

Dr. Dick's itch took him to a lot of places, and one of his favorite venues for finding really nice old guns was the age-old institution of the auction. He monitored auctions all over the Southeast and would travel hundreds of miles to get to a nice Parker shotgun or original Colt .45. If he went to an auction and found a really nice gun, he had deep enough pockets that it was just about a sure thing it was going home with him.

Evander had the same kind of appreciation, but a much more limited budget. Very few of his shotguns and rifles had been bought new. He was a firm believer that the old gun with a little character was more desirable than the latest machine-made gun with a fancy finish, stamped-on engraving and a plastic bowling pin finish on the wood. Almost all his shotguns were 50 or more years old, he liked American and English guns. His rifles were mostly pre-'64 model 70 Winchesters. He owned more guns than he really needed, and I guess you could say he had the itch; he just did a better job on not scratching than his friend, Dr. White.

On a visit to Morganton, Evander saw a flyer for an auction that was of real interest to him. Both Evander and Dr. Dick White knew Milton Duckworth and had hunted wood ducks with him at his place on Rhodhiss. Milton, a lawyer from an old money family, owned what seemed like half of Burke County, and one of his holdings was a small farm on the north side of Lake Rhodhiss on the Catawba River. There was a beaver pond on the place and in early fall, the wood ducks were as thick as blue-haired ladies at a bingo festival. Evander and Dick hunted there and stayed at Milton's place on Lake James several times. Milton was moving to Montana to retire, and the auction was to be held in a tent in front of Milton's law office.

There were quite a few nondescript guns in the auction catalogue along with various vehicles, a duck boat and two tractors, but the object of Evander's interest was a Birmingham Small Arms waterfowl gun. It was a big, 3 inch chambered, boxlock with 32 inch barrels and weighed about eight and a half pounds. Both Evander and Dick had admired it when they'd hunted with Milton. It wasn't that the gun was a collector piece; it was just such a great duck gun. Evander wanted the gun and since it was the 21st of March and the auction was on the 19th of April, he had some time to figure out how to keep Dr. Dick from outbidding him.

Evander called Milton's office to try to buy the gun before the auction, but Milton wasn't there. He talked to one of the lawyers working for Milton, but he wouldn't take the responsibility for selling the gun since he didn't know the real value and no one wanted to incur Milton Duckworth's wrath. Evander decided he would just continue to try to get in touch with Milton and kept his mouth shut about the auction, hoping Dick White wouldn't find out. After all, he had almost a month to get the gun from Milton.

Dr. Dick and the Auction

Evander had no luck in contacting Milton, and when he saw Dick a few weeks later at the gun club, his heart dropped when the doctor asked if he had seen the flyer on Milton's auction yet. "That auction's coming up pretty soon. You want to ride up there together?" Dick asked.

"Sure," Evander replied, forcing his grimace into a smile, "that'll work great; we can take my truck; I'll call you and we'll set it up."

"There's a K22 Smith and Wesson in the auction I want and that BSA shotgun's in the auction, too. Man, that's a nice gun." As the words came out of Dr. Dick's mouth, Evander started working on his plan.

About a week before the auction, Evander called Dick up. "Hey, I just thought I'd call and we'd figure when we were going to leave on the 26th. The auction starts at 9:00, if we leave at 6:30 we can stop and you can buy my breakfast." Evander continued, "I just talked to Bob Craft, and he says the stripers on the Albemarle Sound are biting so good you have to hide behind the boat console to bait your hook. I've got something going on next week and can't go, but he said to call him and you guys could fish together this weekend."

Dick was delighted. "You sure you can't go? We could ride together." There was disappointment in Dick's voice, and Evander felt a twinge of guilt.

"Na, I've got to be somewhere else, and I can't get out of it. You guys just go and have fun. Bring me a couple of big ones back for the freezer." Evander was developing a degree of confidence.

On the 26th, Evander was in Dick's driveway at 6:30 as promised. When they stopped for breakfast, he insisted on paying the tab; when they arrived at Milton Duckworth's law offices, there was no tent. "Do you think they moved the auction?" Dr. Dick muttered, dismayed.

Evander shifted uncomfortably in his seat, "Let's go in and find out," his voice sounded nervous.

When they walked in, Milton's secretary, Frances, greeted them with a smile. "Did they move the auction site?" Dick stammered.

Frances looked surprised, "Why, the auction was last week. I just thought you'd come up here to pick up the pistol Mr. Pritchart bought for you."

Dr. Dick turned to his devious friend, shook his head and sighed, "I wondered why you volunteered to drive and then bought my breakfast. Did you get a good deal on the shotgun?"

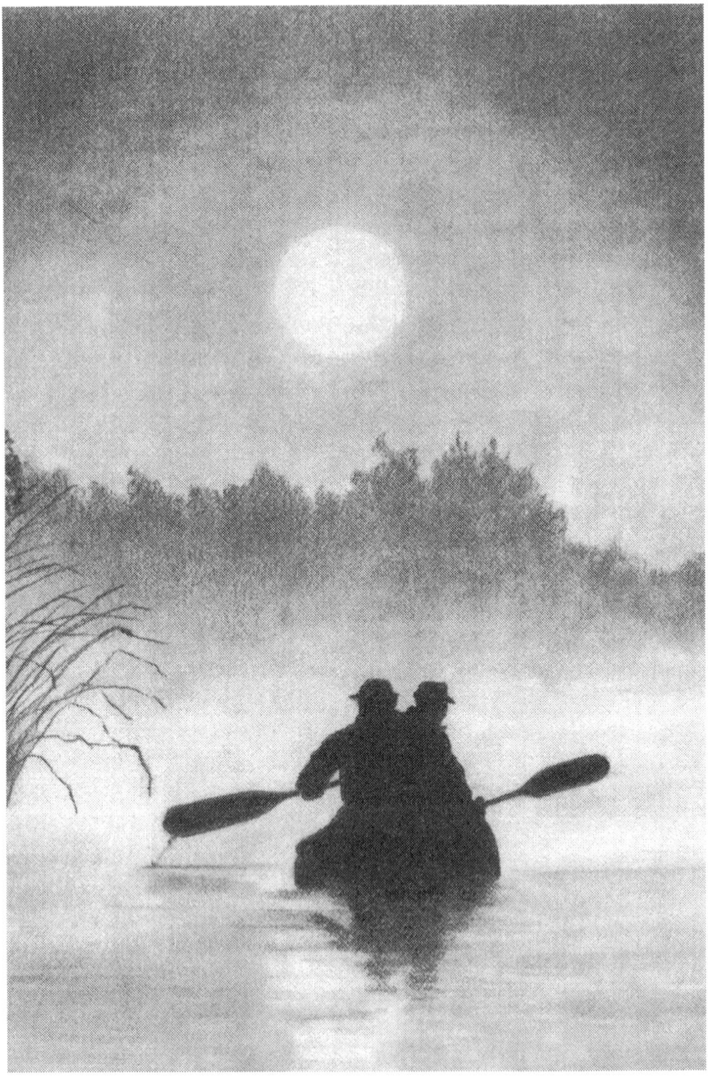

Duck Fever

I sat quietly in the front of the canoe while my Uncle Evander paddled. My eyes worked like a radar screen scanning the river banks from one side to the other from about 75 yards out and back to almost beside the canoe. I was peering out through a screen of Johnson grass, Evander's favorite camouflage material. He was probably responsible for most of the Johnson grass that plagues farmers today because he said it made the best stuff to grass a boat or blind. He had a field of it just for that use and was proud of his stand of the aggravating stuff.

I've always loved floating small rivers and creeks for wood ducks in October. This was the kind of hunting that made me fall in love with waterfowling. In North Carolina, that early October season comes the same time as the Dixie Classic fair. The evenings are clear and cool, the mornings have just a touch of a bite, and sunup and sundown are bathed in wondrous, golden, autumn light.

The serenity of a canoe drifting at a pace just faster than the current mixed with that golden light is sensory overload for me. Combine it with a strong

Duck Fever

anticipation of the fall hunting season, and I'm in heaven. Our fall season really starts with dove season, but dove hunts are like a gaudy party; lots of people and dogs running around, laughter and back slapping. An early fall duck float is like meditation in church with quiet organ music in the background.

The little canoe looked like a floating brush pile from the front with the Johnson grass and other twigs and vegetation Evander had carefully arranged while we waited on a sandbar for an hour and a half before legal shooting hours. We'd been floating on the river now for about twenty minutes and had seen nothing so far. That statement wasn't really true. We'd seen a beaver moving silently across the river in front of us. We'd seen a small deer getting an early drink from a rocky bar, and I'd spent a few minutes mesmerized by the little tendrils of steam that floated off the water like tiny tornadoes. Swirling ten feet high and only a few inches in diameter, they confirmed the fact there was absolutely no wind since a breath from five feet would have disturbed these tiny storms of wind current.

We must have seen the ducks at the same instant because I heard Evander's whisper as I was inhaling to tell him I saw the ducks. Two vague, wraithlike forms darkened the water about 75 yards ahead, now joined by three more silently dropping in from the fog. They were completely relaxed, having no fear and sensing no danger. I gripped the shotgun a little tighter. I silently took the safety off and put it back on. I was frozen with my eyes focused on the five wood ducks that were now 60 yards away.

Duck fever is normally different from buck fever in that it comes suddenly when an empty sky is suddenly full of ducks with wings cupping and

Duck Fever

dropping into the decoys. When you sneak ducks, it comes like buck fever, slowly and from within. I noticed an increase in pulse. My breathing became constricted. I thought of how silly it was to get so excited about a few little ducks, but now, they were well within shotgun range.

I knew that Evander was working his magic with the canoe. I could feel the power of his strokes, and we were closing on the ducks fast. The floating brush pile that was our canoe was bearing down on them, and they were as relaxed as if they were sitting around after a church picnic. There was nothing to cause them to be alarmed. I was hiding behind the Johnson grass, Evander's hands that were working the paddle were hidden behind me, and the silently sculling paddle was hidden behind the side of the canoe and Evander.

They should have been able to hear my heart by now. They were so close that I could see their eyes and pick out the 3 drakes and 2 hens clearly. We were within the length of the canoe when one of the hens showed alarm. The safety clicked off without conscious effort. The shotgun came to my shoulder in a fluid motion. I picked out the first drake and blocked him out with the barrels. The gun rocked in recoil, and I picked out the next drake and fired again. Opening day, barely sunup, and a double... only it wasn't a double. All five ducks were winging their way down the river totally unscathed. I hadn't cut a feather.

I felt a peculiar vibrating motion in the canoe and heard a strained asthmatic wheezing behind me. Evander's face was red and contorted with laughter. "Good shooting, Dick. You get to paddle now."

We switched off on the next sandbar, him

Duck Fever

getting in the front with a beat up Mossberg pump (he didn't like to tie guns in and said he didn't mind losing the Mossberg), and me in the back with the paddle. I considered myself a pretty good river pilot but as soon as we started out, I was having trouble. The current would swing from one side of the river to the other, and I always seemed to be a stroke behind. I was afraid to switch hands and paddle on the left side because Evander had told me that there was no way to sneak up on ducks when they could see your paddle. I was supposed to keep the canoe pointed to the right bank to allow Evander some angle to shoot, and it seemed it was always pointed to the left bank. At one point, I hit a rock, and the canoe spun around and pointed upriver. I felt the vibration and heard the wheezing again.

Evander turned around and patiently explained the physics involved in keeping a canoe on course down the river for the forty-eleventh time, and I began to do better. Good enough, in fact, to get him close enough to a couple of wood ducks for him to get one, and therefore, getting me back in front with a gun.

It was a great day on the river; perfect weather, a good lunch of Vienna sausages, crackers, and rat cheese and enough ducks that we felt reasonably good about ourselves. After lunch, I got a drake wood duck that flew up the river and almost fell into the canoe when I shot it. I told Evander to find a sand bar so we could switch out again. "Just stay where you are," he said, "I'll keep paddling."

The ducks were wary by now, but he was skillful enough with the paddle that he put me close to the next shot, which I missed. He told me to stay in front and kept paddling. A little later, two drakes got up and flew across the river at a bend, a fairly long but not hard shot; I didn't even mount my gun. "I thought they were too far, but I guess they weren't," I explained. He kept paddling. Next, a wood duck hen got up right next to the boat, and I shot twice and missed. I sighed, "OK, now it's time to switch off."

"Just stay in the front, we're almost to the takeout," he said.

"It's still a mile or so. Why don't you take the front?" I protested.

His expression was level. "Just stay in front, you shoot better than you paddle."

Leave it to Evander to put it in a positive manner. I protested, "I don't think I'm shooting so good."

His face spread into a smile. "I didn't say you were shooting good, I said you shoot better than you paddle!"

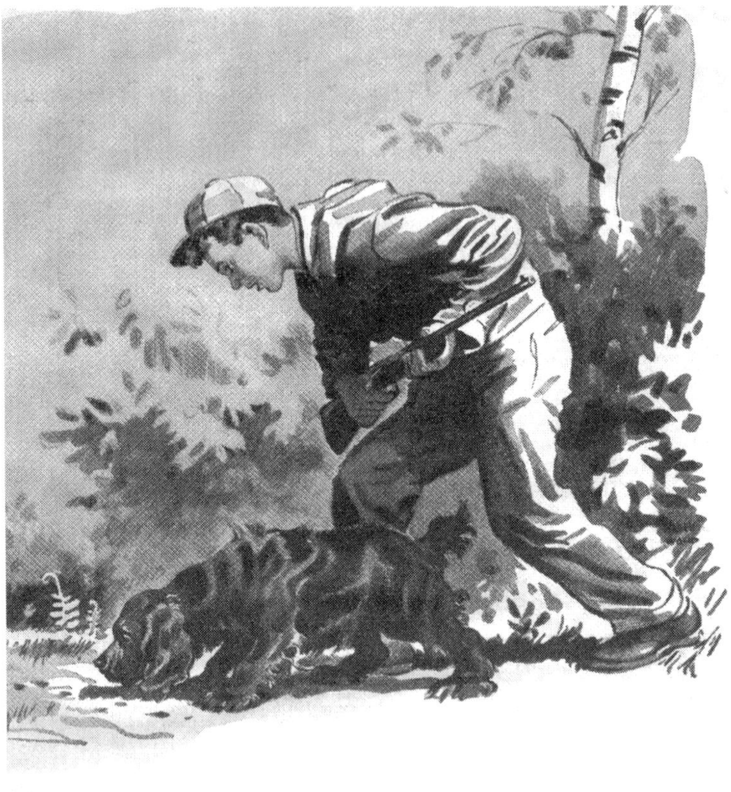

Bill and the Christmas Puppy

Someone once said your life is like a bus. People get on and people get off. Some of those people ride with you a long time because they enjoy riding with you. Those people represent one of the finest things in life, real friendship.

My Uncle Evander had a lot of friends. Most of them had been the recipient of both his kindness and generosity and of his ability to get the best of them in one way or another. Probably, his best friend in the world was Bill Lagle. Bill and Evander had hunted, fished, worked together, shot together, and experienced all sorts of mishaps and near misses with disaster, mostly due to the fact that when they were together, each sort of trusted the other to keep them out of trouble.

Bill had gotten Evander interested in duck hunting and Evander had taken Bill to Cape Hatteras on his first trip for red drum. Bill was a really good shotgunner and Evander was a rifle shooter of some note. They were as different as any two guys that were best friends, but they were so similar in some things that if you talked to one of them, there was no sense in asking advice from the other.

They often wound up driving the same kind of truck or using the same kind of fishing reel, and then, suddenly, the next time you saw them each had an entirely different idea of what was the best truck or fishing reel. If one of them decided he liked something, he'd try to talk the other into buying one, and about half the time it worked. They both agreed that the best boat for them was a Carolina Skiff, but their boats were an entirely different approach to the same purpose.

Most of us go through life never having a friend like that, and Evander often talked about how he realized the value of his friends. He was acutely aware of the things in life that have real importance and friendship was near the top of his list. At the time this conversation happened, I was already a grown man, and I considered Evander to be my best friend. I had the sense to realize that I was not the only person who considered him their best friend. He was a best friend to a lot of people because of how much he did for them. Bill was one of only a few of his friends who did as much for Evander as Evander did for Bill.

Bill's son, Billy, and I were about the same age and we were friends as well, though we didn't see each other often enough to have the same closeness Bill and Evander had. One day when we had just left Bill's house, Evander sighed and said, sort of to me and sort of to no one, "I sure am glad Bill's talking to me again."

I was flabbergasted to think that these two close friends had ever had a serious falling out. "You mean there was a time when you were mad at each other?" I gasped.

"We were never mad at each other but for almost two months, Bill wouldn't speak to me." Evander said softly, like saying it aloud might make the situation come back. "He was really mad, and I guess I deserved it."

He puffed on his cigar absent mindedly and the smoke zipped out instantly as he slightly opened the truck window. "Do you remember old Gunner, Billy's yellow lab? Well I gave him to Billy for Christmas, and if Gunner hadn't turned out to be such a great dog, Bill probably wouldn't be speaking to me now," he said. It took the rest of the trip home, but I heard the story and it's a good one to tell.

Evander had owned a lab named Bob, who happened to be almost the same age as Billy, and Billy loved old Bob. Billy would spend hours playing with Bob when both were younger and as he got older, he wanted a dog of his own. Bill didn't think Billy was ready for the responsibility, but Evander did. When Billy wasn't around, they argued about it for hours. Since old Bob went everywhere Evander went, Evander would think of how nice it would be for Billy to have a great dog like Bob and constantly tried to convince Bill it was a good idea. Bill argued that there was a lot more to it than Evander saw and told him politely to mind his own business.

On the next hunting or fishing trip, the subject would come up again and with the same results. Evander pledged that he would buy the dog and pay the vet bills, but there was no convincing Bill. The running argument would sometimes last the whole length of a fishing or hunting trip, and when it died down, it came up again when something reminded Evander of how Billy would enjoy having his own dog.

Evander was right on this one and once Billy got Gunner, he proved a responsible owner and trainer, reading books on dog training while Gunner was a puppy, and working out every training problem he encountered as Gunner grew. In fact, raising Gunner had a remarkable effect on Billy. He became more responsible about other things as well and matured with the responsibility. Bill had loved Gunner as much as Billy had, and when Billy went off to school, Bill kept him until, like all of our canine companions, he aged faster than his human counterparts. He died and took a little piece of their hearts with him.

As we rode east on Highway 64, and I listened to Evander's story, I just couldn't get my mind around why someone as reasonable as Bill Lagle would have gotten mad over Evander giving Billy this puppy that they both enjoyed so much. "I still don't understand why Bill got so mad at you over Gunner," I mused.

Evander sighed, wiped his hand down his face, as he often did when he was trying to frame a story, and replied. "Well, I guess he wasn't all that mad that I gave Billy the dog as much as how I gave him Gunner. You see, I never convinced Bill that Billy really should have a dog, but when old Bob became a daddy and one of the pups looked just like him, I couldn't let that dog go to someone who wouldn't appreciate him. Bob was old at the time, and I knew it would be the last litter he sired. I just wanted Billy to have one of Bob's pups, and I knew if I didn't give him this one, it would be too late."

Evander's voice grew softer and he savored the story like a butterscotch candy. "It was close to Christmas, and I knew Bill didn't lock his doors, so at 4:00 AM on Christmas morning, I slipped over to their house and left little Gunner in the living room!" Evander chuckled, "I sure am glad Gunner turned out to be a good dog!"

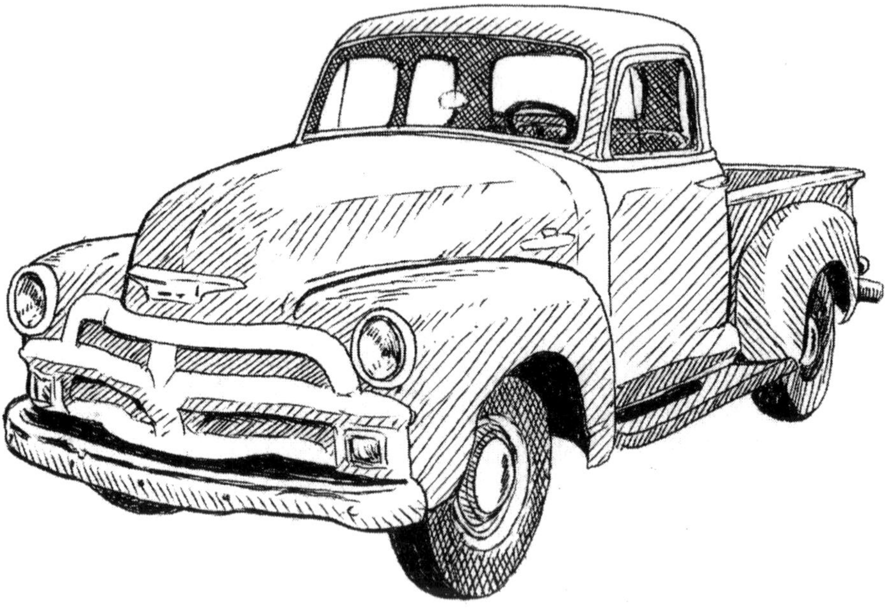

Dr. Dick's New Truck

My Uncle Evander spent a lot of time in his vehicles. He traveled on business, and of course, he went to a lot of places to hunt, fish, and shoot. The things he valued were not luxury items like leather seats but practical things like a comfortable seat and four-wheel drive. He also realized that, if he had a really nice truck, he wouldn't be so cavalier about driving it through a field of briars or a puddle of salt water. He tended not to buy new trucks; he claimed there was a lot of cost involved with "new car smell." The smell of his truck was rarely "new car." It was more likely "stale cigar" or "wet dog;" In fact, when he went to the car wash after the newfangled automated car washes came along, he requested "Wet Labrador Retriever" as the air freshener. The lady at the car wash just nodded and marked down what she wanted to on his windshield.

  The vehicle I remember best was his old, green Chevy pickup. It was several years old when he first got it and it already had been around once on the odometer. It had some rust and the carpet was kind of sticky for some reason but it would go anywhere. Evander didn't believe in big, blocky truck tires with mud lugs; he preferred oversized car tires. They rode better on the highway and, when properly deflated, ran across the loose sand of the Hatteras beaches like they were an A&P parking lot.

The old, green Chevy served as the main component of a collection of attachments that resembled a Mr. Potato Head kit. As you may remember, a Mr. Potato Head kit was a series of ears, noses, eyes, etc., that you could use to accessorize a potato.

Around Evander's old tobacco barn was the Mr. Potato Head kit for the old green truck. There was a lightweight aluminum camper top that he used to protect stuff on trips. It locked and provided a place for old Bob, the Lab, to sleep if the motel had a no pet policy. It had side windows that lifted up to allow Evander to get to what he needed without climbing in from the back, and he packed it carefully to keep himself from having to dig around for what he needed. He also had a little cot that went inside the top to allow him a place to crash. Sometimes when he went to the Roanoke River for the striper run, to save money, he'd sleep in the truck for a couple of days instead of getting a hotel room.

The camper top also had a rack on top for carrying two canoes. Evander loved to float the river to fish, shoot wood ducks, or just to enjoy the river. He even had an attachment for his Old Town canoe that made it a duck hunting canoe; it was a board that was shaped like the bow of the canoe and had holes in it for sticking brush. Once brushed, the canoe looked like a floating brush pile from the front.

There was a combination armrest/storage

Dr. Dick's New Truck

unit/marine radio mount that he used on surf fishing trips. It was made of pine boards and even featured a padded armrest. The marine radio provided communication with his friends in the days before cell phones, and of course, the marine weather report always came in handy. In later years, he included a marine GPS unit that could be unplugged and mounted on the boat when you got to the river. He'd drive up the beach marking surf fishing holes as waypoints or use the search function to find a gunshop to cruise.

There was a rod rack made of PVC pipes that went on a bracket on the front. It had a fold-down rack that held a cooler and 8 vertical pipes for carrying the multiple fishing rods that were required for a trip to the Cape. There were two rod holders that stuck out at a 45 degree angle he used for holding the rod when he changed baits or rigs. A section of six-inch pipe with a faucet carried water for washing your hands.

Of course, the biggest attachment of all was the old slide-in camper that went on the truck. Evander had bought it for $300, and when he and Bill Lagle went to pick it up, he suggested that they both get a tetanus shot first. It was ugly, but I'll admit, it was functional. After Evander and Bill bought it, they found out the roof was in bad shape so they replaced it and over-engineered it so much, it could be used as an observation platform. The inside of the camper contained every imaginable piece of tackle you'd ever need on the beach and had a bed over the cab and a couch that accommodated a guest. Evander never removed the collection of rigs, sinkers, waders, cast nets, bait buckets, sand spikes, rain gear, rods, reels, and all the other stuff

Dr. Dick's New Truck

that was needed for a surf fishing trip. As a result, the old slide-in became the worlds largest tackle box, always sitting there ready to be put on the truck and on the road in less than an hour.

Once, I helped him build one of his projects; a combination back porch for the slide-in camper that would also fit on the boat trailer as a step to make it easier to get on the boat while it was on the trailer. It was a neat invention that slid into the Reese hitch on the truck and also onto a Reese hitch he had attached to the boat trailer. It had a few rod tubes, a small platform area, and a step. It also had a place to secure a small cooler and a little bait-cutting board.

I noticed he was really enjoying building this thing, and I asked why he was having so much fun. "Getting ready for the trip is sometimes as much fun as the trip," he grinned. "I enjoy doing this and I get a kick out of what people say when they see what I've done. It's just part of the fun."

I now think of how the truck looked with the camper and rod rack on it, towing the Carolina Skiff and the long surf rods hanging in the racks on the side. It looked like the Outdoor Action Figures that are sold as toys at Bass Pro Shops. I guess old Evander was an Outdoor Action Figure.

One day, several of Evander's friends were at his house shooting on the shotgun range in the field behind his house when Dr. Dick White drove up in a brand new Range Rover with every bell and whistle you could get. It was a four-wheel drive, ¾ ton, with power everything and chrome everywhere. It looked just like the trucks in Tarzan movies and made in England. Dr. Dick was bragging about how the four-wheel drive could be turned on at the touch

Dr. Dick's New Truck

of a button and how the tires and ground clearance guaranteed he would never get stuck.

Evander admired the truck and then announced, "I'll wager $5,000 that my old, green, truck will go where Dr. Dick's new $25,000 wonder won't."

Dr. Dick's face turned red and he shot back, "I ought to take your money on that one. You know better than that. Where would your truck go that mine wouldn't?"

Evander's arm gestured to the fish pond and his face spread into a smile, "For $5,000 I'll drive my truck into the pond. Will you drive yours into the pond?"

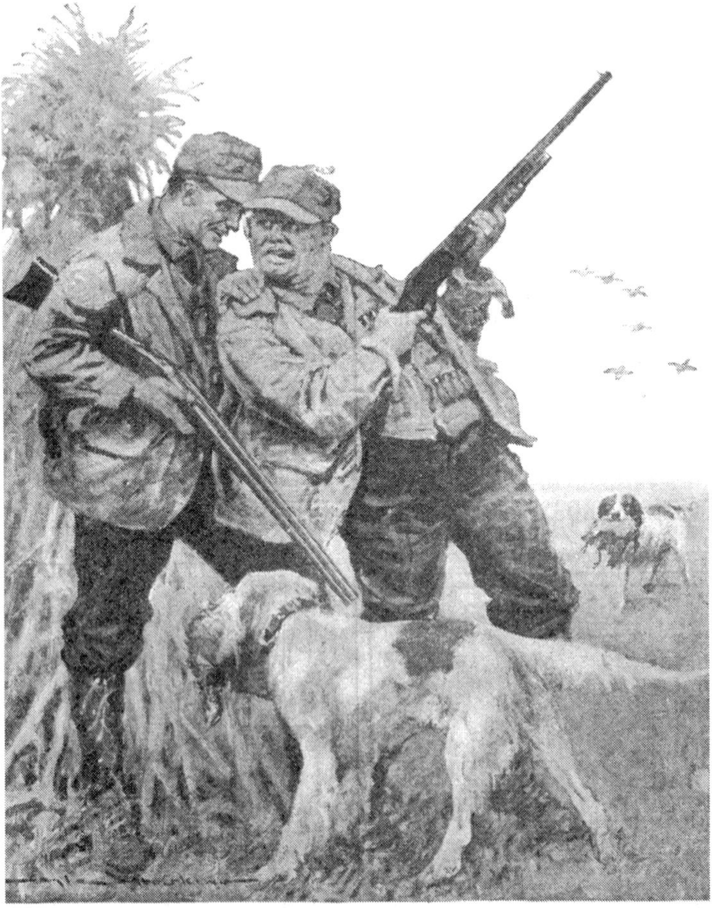

Jake and the Dove Spot

Uncle Evander always dove hunted from the same spot in Bill Lagle's field. There were two cedar trees about thirty feet apart that were on either side of the power line, and Evander sat under one of the cedars for an afternoon hunt since that allowed him to face east, and he sat under the other for a morning hunt which allowed him to face west. He always advised me to hunt doves with the sun to my back. "Doves don't wear sunglasses," he reasoned, "and you're a lot harder to see when you're in the shadows."

He always hunted under one of those two cedars and no one ever tried to get the spot for some reason. Sometimes there was quiet talk about him always taking this choice spot. He was normally the first to limit out, but no one asked him about why he always felt entitled to hunt that spot. On getting his limit, he'd always walk his old Lab, Bob, down to the pond for a cooling-off swim. As he walked by, he'd always invite someone who was having trouble getting their limit to go take the spot. It was probably the best place in the field.

It was such a good spot because the power lines always attracted birds, there was always shade to hide in, and it was next to the road so there was a natural channel for the birds to fly through. He and old Bob would sit under the tree in the shade on his webbed aluminum folding lawn chair. When the doves came in, he'd sit still as a statue until they were in range. He would then stand up and shoot; Bob would run out and get the bird, drop it in the pile, and reposition himself at Evander's left elbow. When the next bird came in, they would repeat the cycle.

As I said, no one ever challenged Evander's right to the spot until Jake McGee started shooting there. Jake was a no-nonsense kind of guy. He was a kind of opposite to Evander. They did the same kind of things but in very different ways. Both of them duck hunted, but Jake only hunted with a couple of guys that reminded me of Jake, all business, no jokes or kidding around. Evander hunted with everybody and kept running pranks and jokes going constantly. Jake hunted hard and no frills. Evander built comfortable blinds with little stoves for comfort and cooked breakfast in the blind after the decoys were set. Jake had nice guns, but they were always the latest autoloaders; Evander shot old doubles and fussed over them like they were his kids. Evander was into what was fun and Jake was into what was business. Jake wasn't unpleasant, he just wasn't fun to be around. I always knew that hunting was fun; with Jake, you just couldn't tell it.

Jake had been shooting doves at Bill's for a couple of years when he asked me why Evander always shot from the same spot. I told him that Evander had always shot there, and nobody else had asked to shoot there. This occurred on opening day. On Labor Day, the next day we hunted, I heard Jake tell one of the other shooters the only reason Evander shot so good was because the birds flew in so close at the spot where he hunted. Later, when we were all eating doves grilled on the old drum that Bill had converted into a cooker, something was said about Evander's getting his limit before anyone else. Jake said anyone could get their limit fast where Evander was shooting, and he didn't smile when he said it.

On the way home in the truck, Evander said nothing about Jake, but he did mention that he was glad that he had forgotten to bring the Sevin dust with him this weekend.

In those days, the first week of Carolina dove season required that shooting begin no earlier than twelve o'clock. This is because in the old days folks would shoot a morning limit, eat lunch, and shoot an afternoon limit. After the first week, for some reason, that is not a problem. I guess it is due to pent up pressure for the fun of shooting birds. Maybe after the first week, the pressure drops a little. I was always glad to see the first week pass; morning hunts are my favorite because they're cooler.

On the next Saturday morning, Evander picked me up in the old, green Chevy truck at five thirty. I'd always tried to jog the old man's memory whenever possible because Evander was absent-minded sometimes, and it gave me a way to be of benefit to him. "Did you bring the Sevin dust?" I asked. "Nope, don't need it today, but thanks for askin," came the reply.

I assumed that whatever the dust was to be used for had been taken care of. He and Bill used Sevin dust all summer in their quest to rid the world of wasps, hornets, and yellow jackets. It also got some occasional agricultural use.

It was still dark when we got to the little grove of oaks we always parked under beside the field. By the time everyone had said "Mornin" to everyone else, it was getting light enough to recognize faces. I could have dropped my gun when Evander said, "Jake, why don't you hunt my spot today? Bob and I will hunt over on the other side of the road."

Jake took the offer with just an "OK." Evander then told him that he'd do better if he shot from the cedar that allowed him to face west. Jake said, "Sure," and that was it. We all looked at each other but in the darkness I couldn't tell much from the expressions.

When the birds started to fly, Jake was the first to shoot. About every third shot, though, he would let a string of cuss words loose. The field was pretty small, and I could hear every word. I thought it might be some way he had of expressing pleasure since I was unfamiliar with seeing him act happy. The birds were everywhere, though Jake did not seem to shoot as well as normal. Evander got his limit first again, and as he passed his old spot, I was amazed to hear him offer the spot he had just left to Jake. I was even more amazed to hear Jake accept. Evander and old Bob headed for the pond for Bob's cool-off swim.

It was a great hunt, and we were all limited out, even me. We were back at the oaks by eight fifteen, and for the first time in my life, I saw Jake McGee smile. "Evander Prichart is the only man I know that can cultivate a yellow jacket's nest in less than a week," he chuckled. Evander laughed and wiped his eyes.

"Oh, I figure they'd been there a while; I first noticed 'em on opening day. I'm just glad I forgot the Sevin dust so you could have a chance to enjoy 'em."

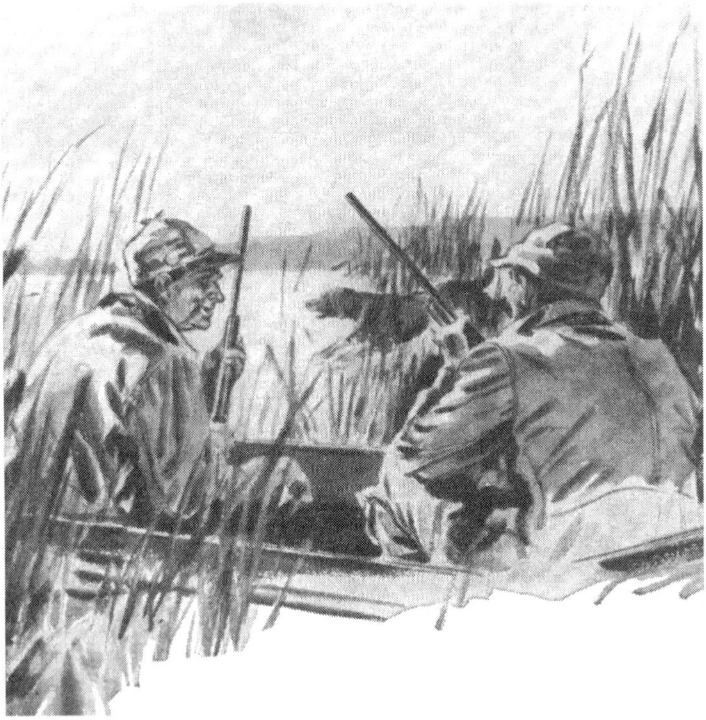

Christmas Duck Hunt

I always loved Christmas as a kid. Sure, there were presents and food, but there was also the time off from school. It was the longest break in the school year, and it always meant time with Uncle Evander.

Uncle Evander had a little house up above Eden, North Carolina, and on my ninth Christmas he came by the house a few days after Christmas Day and had a short meeting with Mom. He had me go outside and play with Bob during the meeting. An old lab like Bob was not the kind of dog you played with, so I knew he was asking for my absence for a while.

He'd given me a pair of hip boots for Christmas and although they were too big, (You'll grow into them he assured me), I was having a ball with them. They were like four wheel drive for a kid. In those days, kids didn't have twenty pairs of shoes in the closet, and you couldn't just go out and mess them up without consequences. I had some awkward rubber boots that had buckles that went over my Sunday or school shoes, but if I got in water over the tops, the shoes under them were wet. The hip boots

Christmas Duck Hunt

were so tall I couldn't imagine how you could get wet feet wearing them. I learned on my next surf fishing trip, but that's another story. I couldn't wait till the next rain storm so I could go out and stomp around in the branch behind the house when it was high.

Evander came out with a grin. "You want to come to my house tonight and go duck huntin' in the mornin'?" I was thrilled. This was why he'd given me the hip boots, and this was the perfect way to break them in. I ran in the house and got my stuff and before he could get Bob in the truck, I was throwing my little bag in the back of the old green Chevy. It was getting dark by the time we got to the end of the dirt road that was our driveway. (It was 3/8 of a mile long and I couldn't imagine what it would be like to live where you could see the paved road.) We stopped at a little diner named Dave's, in High Point, and ate supper. Dave knew Evander and came to our booth to talk to us when he finished what he was cooking. Evander introduced me as if I were a grown man, and they talked about fishing for a while. The waitress was pretty in a kind of dangerous way, and she flirted with my uncle when she took our order. I was tempted to order a plate like Uncle Evander since it was a kind of grown up trip, but I decided on a cheeseburger instead. I wasn't that grown up yet.

We ate our food and while we did, people came up and talked to us. Every time they did, I was introduced as if I was just another guy. I thought this was what it was like to be a grown up bachelor man of the world. When we finished, Uncle Evander said "my treat" just like I could have paid for mine if I had wanted to and left two quarters on the table for a tip, I'd never seen that done before and received an education on the process during the drive to the house.

We went to bed as soon as we got home. I noticed a whole pile of stuff piled in the hall, ready to be loaded into the truck in the morning. It looked as if we were going to be out for a couple of days from the size of the pile, but I didn't ask questions. I slept on the couch as one of my uncle's friends named Bill Lagle was there, and he was sleeping in the bedroom I usually slept in.

The next morning felt like midnight to me. It was four o'clock when Bill turned on the light and started the coffee. I got dressed and put on two pairs of socks under my hip boots. I noticed that there was no breakfast cooking but didn't ask. The coffee was poured into thermos bottles, and we turned out the lights and left the house. Bill hitched the little Carolina boat to Evander's old, green truck and with Bob in the back and with me between Evander and Bill we pulled out of the driveway. I figured we'd stop at a café and have some breakfast, but the next place we stopped was the public boat ramp at the local reservoir. I still didn't say anything, but I thought that I was going to get pretty hungry by the time we got back.

That boat ramp was one of the darkest places I ever saw. Bill and Evander both had little flashlights on strings around their necks, but they never turned them on. They did everything as if it was broad daylight, and I could hardly see my hand in front of my face. "How do ya'll do that without lights?" I asked as they walked around putting the plug in the boat, hooking up the running lights, and loading everything that had been in the pile in the hall into the little skiff.

"We know where everything is, and we just feel for it," Bill answered. "That's why it's important to keep things where they belong." I thought of how many times Evander had told me to, always, put things back where I got them, and for the first time, it made real sense.

It was a warm morning for late December, probably about thirty-five degrees, but when Evander revved up the little Johnson motor and put the boat on plane, the cold was so instant and intense it took my breath away. I didn't say anything, but I snuggled up to Bob and turned my face away from the wind as best as I could.

When the boat slowed, Bill flipped on his flashlight enough to expose what looked like a hog shed built in a brush pile on the bank, and Evander beached the boat and cut the motor. Once again, work commenced in impenetrable dark as Bill and Evander unloaded the pile of stuff and put it into the blind. "Dick, you can get warmed up by helping us with the decoys," Evander said. I didn't realize that he had even noticed the cold until then.

Bill opened the hatch in the bow of the boat, and instead of the fishing gear that I'd always seen there, it was now full of decoys. Bob lay down on the bank in front of the blind to supervise and with me in the boat and the men in the water, we pushed back into the lake. I pulled the decoys from the box and unwrapped the lines. I got the impression that it would have been faster without my help, but I never noticed any impatience on the part of Evander and Bill.

Then there was considerable discussion of the placement of the decoys and the stringing of the diver line (a string of decoys that worked like a trot

Christmas Duck Hunt

line), then more discussion of the proper way to set the pull line. This was a line with three decoys on a kind of rubber band that could be pulled from inside the blind. It looked so real that I kept thinking it was real ducks all morning.

Finally all this work was done, and I realized I wasn't cold anymore. Evander and I went to the blind, and Bill went to hide the boat. It was still pitch dark, and while I understood the principle of hawking hours from past conversations, I assumed that my hosts had made a miscalculation in timing. I found out this was not the case when Evander pulled out a small stove and laid out breakfast. Everyone and his brother has talked about how food is always better outdoors, but when it's cold, on the water, and dark, the smell of sausage in a frying pan is like nothing else I've experienced. By the time Bill was back from hiding the boat, we had sausage, eggs and bread fried in butter and slathered with blackberry jelly from Mom's basement. I had coffee, black, with mine. It was the first black coffee I ever tried, and while it was too strong to drink while I was eating eggs and sausage, it provided a surprisingly pleasant contrast for the fried bread and jelly.

Bill and Evander cleaned up the cooking stuff, put it away, and prepared for battle. Shotgun shells were laid out on the little shelf in the blind, duck calls were checked and I was instructed not to move when told to be still. Bill pulled out a Winchester pump with a hammer. I'd never seen such a strange looking gun. Evander uncased his old silver-sided Sterlingworth Fox.

We only killed four ducks that day, all ringnecks. Evander said they weren't very good to eat, but we had them for supper that night anyway.

Christmas Duck Hunt

They were breaded and fried, then slow cooked in gravy. I thought they were as good as anything I'd ever eaten. The shooting I don't really remember. What I do remember was how the ducks came by like jets and the way you could hear them before you saw them. I can still hear the sound of those wings. Not like any other sound I have ever heard. It was kind of like some strange wind water sound, but really, words don't work for things like that.

We were off the water by noon, and the stuff was all cleaned up and put away by the two men. Kids are selfish, and I was no different. I complained that I'd not really gotten to use my waders as I'd stayed in the boat during the decoy setting and picking up. Evander laughed and said that I should be worn out by now, but if I wasn't we could go for a walk. He put on rubber boots, and I put on my hip boots. He showed me how to put my pants inside my socks to keep them from rolling up and how to hook the loops of the boots on my belt to keep them from falling down. We walked through the little bog behind his house that seemed like a swamp to me. He showed me deer tracks, coon tracks, and scat, and spotted a huge owl sitting on a tree limb not twenty yards from us. I was amazed at how big and quiet the bird was, when he got nervous and flew off. We went to an old cemetery where the graves were dated into the 1700s, and he explained to me what life was like for the people buried beneath our feet. We went to two old falling-down ruins of houses from days so far past that no one he knew remembered who'd lived there. When we walked back and got to the yard, I was too tired to complain when he suggested that I lie down and rest before supper.

Other than how good those ringnecks

tasted for supper, I don't remember that evening or anything else that happened on that trip, but every time I sit in a duck blind and hear those wings or eat breakfast cooked in the wild, I remember how I felt like a man that trip, and he's right there with me.

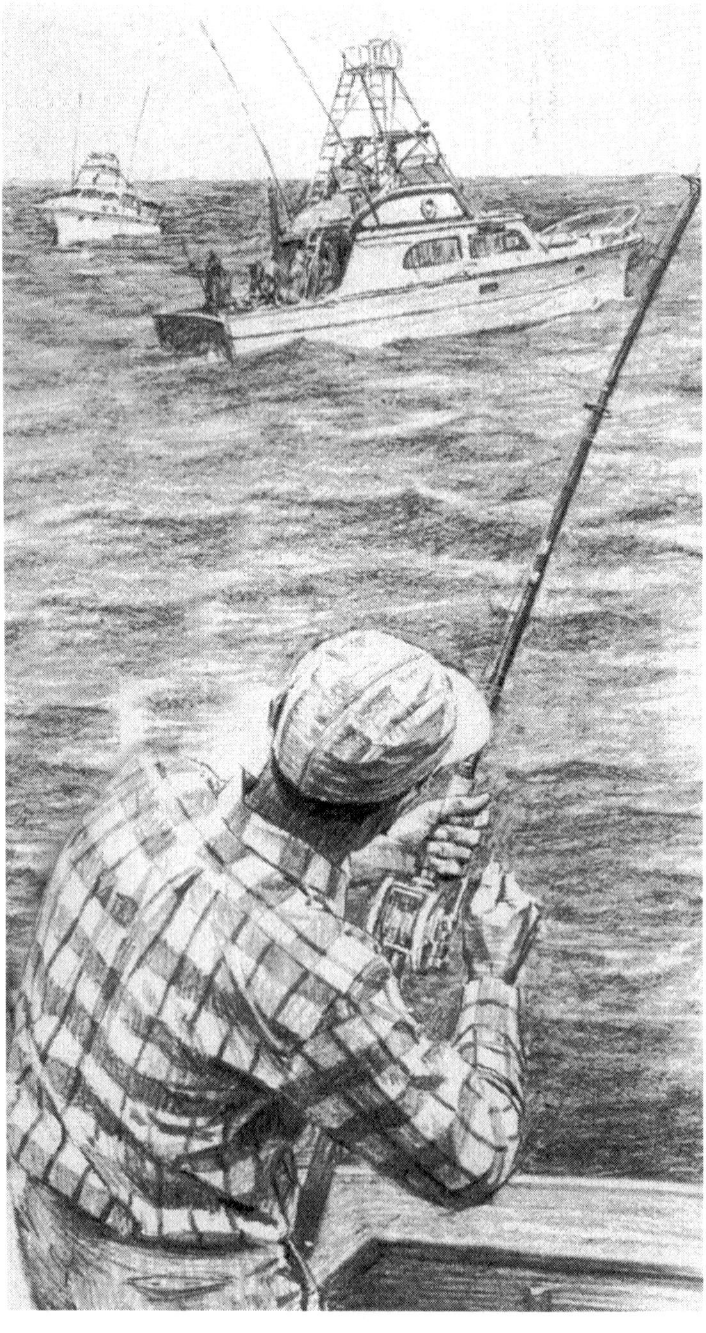

Doc and the Big School of Drum

My Uncle Evander was a busy man. On this particular morning, he'd gotten up at sunrise to fish the high tide from the Point of Cape Hatteras, met a friend for breakfast and helped another friend repair a duck blind in the sound. I'd fished with him, and then gone back to the motel room to cover some troublesome schoolwork that had been a precondition to my being able to go on the trip. He promised me we'd go out in the skiff in the afternoon to look for Fat Alberts. Fat Alberts is the Hatteras Island slang name for false albacore.

In late October and early November, the Fat Alberts came around the hook of Cape Hatteras and bullied up the neighborhood. False albacore are of no value for the table, but I'm sure that the manufacturers of fishing reels appreciate them because they're known as reel wreckers. I know I valued finding and catching them highly since they were the meanest fish pound for pound that I'd ever caught.

On bluebird days, as Evander called them, we'd take the 19 foot Carolina Skiff out and run up and down the beach looking for birds and what is best described as the appearance of machine gun bullets hitting the water. Normally what we found was bluefish. That was OK, but sometimes we hit the jackpot and got into the Alberts. We'd seen them off the Point and out of range of even the longest casters during the morning surf fishing, and I'd begged my uncle to take me out there then. His philosophy was that a promise was a promise, and he'd committed the morning to helping one friend with a blind and going to breakfast with another. I did schoolwork and went crazy. I could just imagine those fish....

Finally, I heard the old, green Chevy truck pull into the parking lot and I jumped up and started getting ready. I was more hindrance than help in getting the trailer hooked up, but Evander always made me do my share of the project. We stopped to fill the boat up with gas, and Evander wound up talking to the owner of the service station, and acting like we had all the time in the world. I fidgeted.

When we arrived at the boat ramp, Evander backed the trailer in as smooth as a trucker with fifty years of experience and let me handle the boat while he parked the trailer. As I awkwardly negotiated the boat up to the side of the dock, I noticed Dr. Dick White cleaning his gleaming white center console. Wow, what a boat. With twin outboards, shiny fiberglass and teak, it was the prettiest boat in the harbor. Dr. White had the boat up in the lift and was brushing off the bottom. As I watched, he finished brushing, rinsed off the hull, and began stowing the hose and brush in the teak dock box he kept his boat cleaning stuff in.

"The boat really looks nice, Dr. White," I said, wishing that my uncle had such a nice boat.

Doc and the Big School of Drum

"Thanks, son" he beamed. "It takes time to keep a vessel ship-shape, but it's worth the time. I spend about an hour and a half cleaning her up every time I use her," he said. About that time Uncle Evander finished talking with the stranger that had contributed to delaying our getting out on the water even longer and came up to the boat.

For some reason, there always seemed to be a certain amount of tension between my uncle and Dr. Dick White. They always seemed to have some sort of running conflict. Dr. Dick sometimes scoffed at the bluefish and albacore Evander enjoyed catching. He would joke that Evander was a "bottom feeder" since he'd fish for anything that was biting. Dr. Dick liked to fish for red drum and stripers with a fly rod. Evander always said Dr. Dick was a "purist".

"Hey Prichart," Dr. Dick shouted over the rattle of Evander's outboard, "tell me a big fish lie."

Evander hardly looked up from the controls as he steered the boat out of the little harbor. "I don't have time now, Doc. I just found out that there's a big school of drum just off the point, and I want to get to 'em before they leave." We motored out of the harbor with the Doctor standing with his jaw slack.

A nineteen foot Carolina Skiff is not a fast boat under any conditions. My uncle saw his skiff as a sort of four wheel drive boat. He could go anywhere that any boat, except an airboat, would go since the skiff had a jackplate that raised the motor even more than it already was. It would float in ankle deep water and get up on plane in water that wouldn't come to your knees. He joked that it would follow a sweaty mule up a dirt road. Boats are all about compromise, however, and the things that made his old skiff work well in shallow water conspired against it in swells. It was unsinkable but slow in relation to the fast boats that were meant for running in the ocean.

As we negotiated the serpentine course that led out to the inlet, Evander kept looking back over his shoulder. As we rounded the last turn before the inlet, he looked back and chuckled to himself. This was not that unusual for him because he was constantly chuckling at things that I didn't see as funny at all.

He didn't talk much on the way to the Point; he just studied the sky and occasionally checked behind us. As we approached the point, I saw the birds and the tell-tale machine gun traces on the water. We came up within a hundred yards or so of the fish and he stopped to check the wind direction. He motored around to a spot upwind of the fish so the wind would drift us past the line the fish were taking. He cut the motor.

"OK boy, get ready, we are about to tangle with Albert. Looks like Doc decided to join us." There was a little too much going on for me to follow it all.

"I thought we were going after those drum," I said, thoroughly puzzled.

"The albacore are right on us, let's fish for albacore," he grunted as his rod bent and the drag on his little red Ambassadeur reel sang. The excitement was too much for me, and I fumbled the first cast into a little backlash. I cleared it, cast again, and connected. Wow, this was fun, drum or no drum.

As I played my fish, I saw Dr. Dick had set up a drift and connected with a fat Albert, too. Evander played his fish while he negotiated the boat away from the shoals and the school of fish. As we were releasing the first two fish, Dr. Dick drifted close as he boated his fish.

"Where are the drum?" he shouted, over the rattle of our outboard.

"What drum?" Evander asked.

"I put my boat back in the water after cleaning it up because you said there was a big school of drum out here!" he shouted.

"Oh, there weren't any drum, Doc" Evander answered. "I just told you that 'cause you asked me to tell you a big fish lie!"

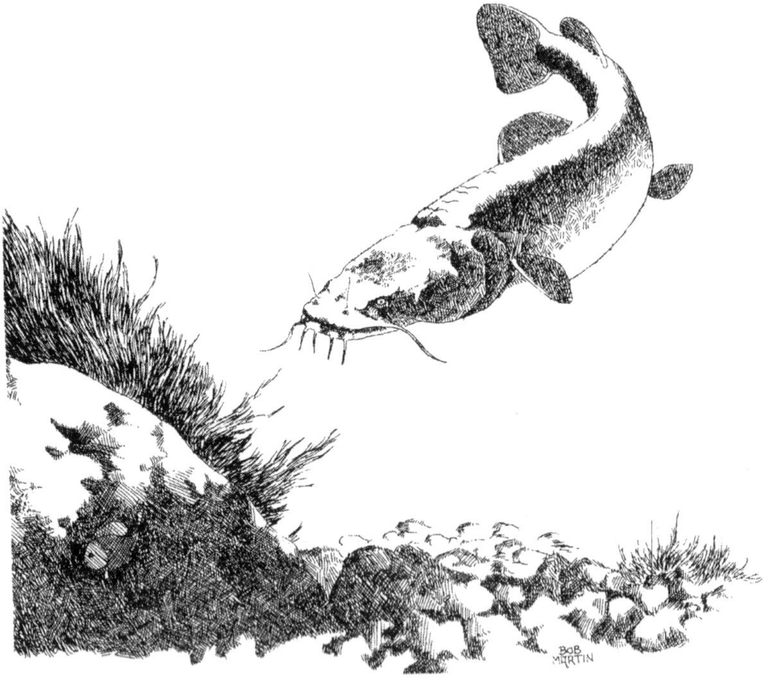
BOB
MARTIN

Everything Grows Fast in Summer

The feeling that came with getting out of elementary school for the summer has no comparable emotion when you're an adult. Now that I'm past 60, summer is my least favorite time of year. The older I get, the more the heat saps the energy out of me. As a younger man, I could stay out on the rifle range all day, with practically no shade, and lie down in a heavy leather coat to shoot while the sun cooked the full length of my body. Now I suffer in the shade with a light shirt and shorts.

That last day of school was so sweet that I don't even remember thinking about how hot it was. Oh sure, I noticed the heat when I was hoeing tobacco or chopping the grass out of the field of corn that we put in the corn crib in the fall to feed old Dolly, the mule. Mowing the yard was another time that the heat made me suffer, but when I was doing fun stuff, shooting my BB gun, having corn cob fights in the barn loft, or playing Tarzan in the woods, (I've got some really good stories about swinging on grape vines.) I had so much fun, I never even noticed it was hot.

Everything Grows Fast in Summer

There were various cooling-off activities we engaged in. Most of them are not even imaginable by most modern kids. Some, like how Granddad would put a bunch of us kids in the back of his '60 Ford pickup and take us for a ride, would get you arrested. I guess we were pretty unsophisticated to get excited about riding around in the back of a pickup, and I know it was dangerous, but it was great fun at the time.

Going swimming in the creek was fun, too. The only bad part was when the swimming was over and you had to get back in the car with muddy feet from walking up the bank. The first time I swam in a swimming pool, I thought it was wonderful to go through the swimming experience without dealing with the mud.

Of course, the best part of summer was the fishing. About every couple of weeks, Uncle Evander would come over to the house and "borrow" me to take me fishing. Sometimes, we just drove to someone's farm pond, bumping along the little roads that ran through the tobacco fields and fished for bass and bream. These trips happened in the late afternoon. I didn't realize it at the time, but the summer difficulty that I'm feeling nowadays must have affected Evander then, since all those trips happened either early or late, never in the heat of the day.

Of all summer activities, night time catfishing trips were my favorite. They involved multiple exciting activities: fishing, camping, and outdoor eating. The fishing part is obvious; the camping came from the fact that we fished on the side of the river and stayed out all night long. There were no tents or sleeping bags, just old quilts that would now probably bring about $300.00 in an antique store. The eating involved hot dogs cooked on a stick, Mama's fried apple pies, and snacks like Vienna (pronounced VI-EE-NEE) sausages, potted meat, and rat cheese.

There was also live entertainment in the form of stories and discussions between Evander and the various friends that tagged along. One of my favorites was Bob Craft. Bob was a furniture salesman who traveled all over the country and had a million tales to tell. Bob was a sophisticated fellow, wearing clothes like Jungle Jim with double shirt pockets with flaps on the pockets. He sometimes wore a pith helmet. He smoked cigars that were handmade in Honduras and one cigar probably cost as much as a box of the Tampa Nuggets Evander smoked. He was a man of the world compared to the circles I moved in, and though I heard many of his stories more than a time or twelve, they were always interesting. Sometimes, the weight of the bass varied a pound or two and the number of points on the buck increased or decreased depending on his mood, but the stories were good.

One particular evening, we had a pretty good crowd on the river bank. My friend from church, David Magee, his younger brother, Rick, and their Dad, Bill, showed up. David and Rick were both a little younger than me. On this night, Bob was elegantly loquacious, telling all sorts of stories since he had an audience who hadn't previously heard his material. In the process of telling a story about shooting wild chickens on a deer hunt, he nearly lost his Zebco to a huge catfish.

The fish turned out to be about as big a catfish as we'd ever caught on one of these trips, and there

Everything Grows Fast in Summer

was a lot of conjecture about how much it might weigh. The little hand-held scales that everyone has now didn't exist in those days. The fish started out with Bob's guess of 25 pounds. It grew to 28 and then 30 before David, Rick, and Bill went home.

The next Saturday I was having breakfast with Bob and Evander at Wahoo's Restaurant when Bill, his wife, Shelby, David, and Rick walked in. Bob asked them to join us for breakfast and proceeded to tell Shelby the story of the big catfish he had caught last week. By now, the fish was up to 38 pounds. Bob could tell a story, and several tables close to us asked questions after he reached the climatic end of the story.

All things have to come to an end, and eventually, that wonderful summer gave its last gasp, and we returned to the sweaty, early part of the school year. On a late dove hunt in October, David and Bob met again. After the hunt, the dove breasts were roasting on the grill wrapped in bacon. David and I had succumbed to the temptation of eating hotdogs right off the grill with no bun or dressings, and Bob was telling another story.

He was describing the sailfish he'd recently landed in Mexico, and how the sail fish is the fastest growing fish known to science, growing to maturity in just a few years. David, with a mouthful of a Jesse Jones hotdog, interrupted him by saying that he knew of a fish that grew faster.

Bob's head snapped around wide-eyed and surprised. "No," Bob explained patiently, "a sail-fish is the fastest growing fish. What fish grows faster?"

David looked serious, "Mr. Bob, that catfish you caught last June gained 13 pounds in less than a week!"

I Learn About
Insect Control

Kermit Ellis was the slowest man I ever knew. The first time I met Kermit, it was late summer, and we were in an obscure area of North Carolina known by the locals as Lick Skillet. He was in his hammock on the front yard at his house. Beside the hammock was a little folding table with a pack of Winstons, a Zippo lighter, and a sweaty glass of iced tea. I'd never seen anyone talk so slow. I assumed at first that he was talking slow to keep the considerable volume of tobacco juice he was carrying from leaking out.

I'd ridden with Uncle Evander over to his house to inquire about dove hunting. We'd gone to Kermit's house with a definite purpose, but to hear my uncle talk, we'd just happened to be driving down the road, saw Kermit on the hammock, and decided to stop and see how he was doing.

Evander and Kermit discussed everything from butterbeans to motorcycles while I sat in an aluminum lawn chair and rubbed the ears of a farm dog I later learned was named Susie. I was young then, and I was irritated by all this discussion of tractor batteries and bench grinders that continued

I Learn About Insect Control

on for what seemed like an eternity. "Have ya'll had supper yet?" Kermit inquired.

"No, we hadn't, but we didn't come for a free supper," Evander replied. I rolled my eyes internally since my uncle had gone to great lengths to describe the quality of food that Ethel, Kermit's wife, always put on the table.

City people always describe meat when they talk about southern country cooking. They discuss hams and fried chicken. They think of mashed potatoes and biscuits and iced tea. They think of the food that's sold in restaurants as country cooking, and don't get me wrong, that kind of food is good. The things that they don't know about are homemade light rolls, pinto beans, sliced tomatoes, real creamed corn (not anything like what you get in a restaurant), colored butterbeans, and what we called stewed potatoes. Mashed potatoes were for Sundays when the preacher came. Stewed potatoes were the staple of life. They were chunks of potatoes cooked in water and butter until the water used to cook them became a kind of potato soup. They always had to have a generous extra shaking of black pepper added because the women of the house were a little too timid with it. When combined with a few of the above entrees and perhaps some fried okra, you would forget that there was no meat on the table.

We ate meat more in the winter when there was not so much distraction from those fresh vegetables. I know a lot of outdoor guys aren't real big on vegetables, and I wouldn't blame them knowing what the stuff that comes out of a can tastes like. I don't remember what Ethel put on the table that evening, but I remember I noted that when Evander

I Learn About Insect Control

came over here the next time, I wanted to go if it was close to suppertime. I ate like a pig and must have put away six or eight light rolls. I finished up by sopping up the juice from the beans, corn, and potatoes with one more roll. Most of this food had been out in the garden last night and had ridden to the Ellis household on the back of Kermit's motorcycle in a milk crate before the dew had time to dry.

I did discover that the tobacco juice was not the contributing factor in the slowness of Kermit's speech. He talked just as slow without it and he ate slow, too. In fact, he drank tea slow and later, when we went out on the porch for his Winston and Evander's cigar, he even lit his cigarette slow. He pulled the cigarette slowly from the pack, fished for a match, struck the match on his overall button and slowly inhaled the smoke. He very efficiently used the exhale cycle to blow out the match in a cloud of rich smoke.

About halfway through the cigar, Evander finally brought up the reason for the visit. By this time I'd pretty much forgotten it, and it surprised me a little. By now, I was enjoying the stories and had gotten distracted. In case you're wondering what part I'd played in this conversation, it was very little. In those days when a young man accompanied an old man, the young man's place was to answer questions, compliment the wife's cooking, and appear modest when complimented on what a fine man he was going to turn out to be.

"Any doves around here?" Evander slid the question in as though he hadn't thought of doves in two months. I detected a twinkle in Kermit's eye, though it could have just been my imagination.

I Learn About Insect Control

"We primed the fields (pulled tobacco) along the road yesterday and there were doves all over the power lines when I came back from the backer barn," Kermit replied. He seemed to be watching me. "Why? Are you going to want to hunt this year?" he drawled.

Uncle Evander now seemed to twinkle a little, and I suspected that there was a joke going on that I didn't have enough information to get.

Kermit continued without waiting for a response. "The season starts next Saturday; I'll have a watermelon cooling for when you get done."

Kermit was not much of a dove hunter. That Saturday was the only time I saw him dove hunt. He came up with a nice old Fox Sterlingworth, shot a few birds, and talked to us. Susie sat beside him but made no effort at retrieving birds. She was a farming dog, not a hunting dog.

There's a little gnat in the south that likes to buzz in your face when you're sweaty. They do you no physical harm, but the effect on one's sanity is another matter. Doves are small in the distance and a tiny gnat at three inches looks remarkably like a dove at fifty yards. They can be nerve-wracking.

Kermit sat next to me for a few minutes and watched me twitch as they came across my field of vision. "Dick," he drawled, his voice gurgling with tobacco juice. "If you'll go to the house and bring back a jug of ice water, I'll tell you how to keep them dog pecker gnats out of your face."

I knew I was being baited, but I was really thirsty and I agreed. I trotted the few hundred yards to the back door of the house. At my request, Ethel filled a quart mason jar with water and ice, wrapped it in a towel, and gave me a little basket to carry it

I Learn About Insect Control

in. I drank my water at the house since I felt I should offer the water to Kermit first, him being the host and my senior. I also didn't relish the thoughts of drinking Red Man Chewing Tobacco-flavored ice water.

When I got back he offered me a drink first, spit some juice, and drank off about half of the quart without putting it down. "Cut a hole in the seat of your britches," he drawled.

"What?" I looked at him thinking I had misunderstood.

He smiled and said clearly and even more slowly than normal, "I told you I'd tell you how to keep them gnats out of your face."

He chuckled, and his eyes looked mischievous. "If you cut a hole in the seat of your britches, the gnats won't buzz around in your face."

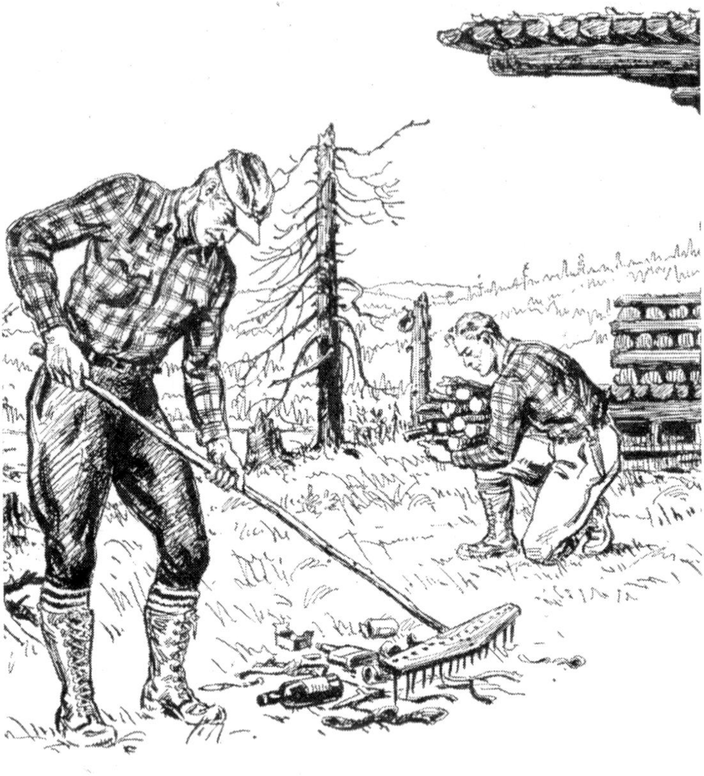

Evander's Deer Club Goes to Work for Big Bucks

The Wallburg Diner was the kind of place where friendships are strengthened, plans are made, and conspiracies are forged. Wallburg, a tiny little town on NC 109, was one of Evander's favorite municipalities. The town had two parking spaces at the post office, one regular and one handicapped. It was a small town. Evander had a lot of friends from Wallburg, and it was the kind of place he liked. Evander was an open-hearted person, but there was one thing he despised, an urban mindset. He believed people were meant to talk to each other and have real concern for each other's problems. He also believed they should share in each other's joys. Wallburg was that kind of town.

The Wallburg Diner kind of epitomized what rural living should be like to him. I know this because he told me. We'd go to the diner for breakfast when he didn't have urgent business like fishing or working a dog, and when he stepped through the door, his mood brightened. The proprietor in those days was Red Haymore. I assume Red got the name from his red hair, but I never knew it to be anything but white. Red always had a serious look on his face, though he never really seemed to me to worry about anything. He seemed to me more like a kindly old preacher than a restaurateur, but maybe not. Most of the time, Red was wearing Big Mac bib overalls.

The fare at the diner was nothing special. There would be three or four meats, a dozen or so vegetables, and corn bread and rolls for lunch. Of course there were also hotdogs, hamburgers, and grilled pimento cheese sandwiches. Breakfast was the number one reason for dining at Red's establishment, though. Eggs and crisp bacon, homemade biscuits, and huge slices of country ham graced the Formica-topped booth tables. My favorite was biscuits and gravy. For a buck, twenty-five, you got two big biscuits smothered in some of the best gravy you ever sopped, and there were real sliced tomatoes on the edge of the plate when Red could get them out of his garden.

Margret Everhart was Red's star waitress. She was the kind of person who makes you feel like family whether you are or not. She always had a smile; she would always laugh at your joke, and if you had a hard luck story, Margret would listen to you, making you feel she'd be praying for you for the rest of the week. She always got you what you ordered, and you never ran out of Coca-Cola or coffee.

One morning, while Margret kept everyone's coffee hot, Evander, Mac Drummond, a close friend of my Uncle Evander, and Mel Lohr, the president of Evander's deer club, had a conversation that may have led to the invention of the game camera. Mac was a forerunner around here in the development of deer management. He had a farm in Virginia, near Martinsville, and was always an avid deer hunter. He read a story in Field and Stream about a hunt club called the Cortland County Deer Club, in upstate New York, that planted plots of beneficial plants to improve the quality of its deer herd. These pioneers of deer management even culled undesirable-looking bucks to improve the quality of the herd. Mac was so impressed, he called the magazine to get the address of the club, and they began correspondence. Mac learned a lot about deer management from the Cortland County Deer Club, and he began to share information with Mel and Evander.

The New York club naturally had larger deer since northern deer are genetically a lot larger than our southern whitetails, but the members up there could see a real difference in their herd in just a few years. Mac was on the phone with them every week or so about something, and they invited him to visit if he got the chance.

My Uncle Evander was a close friend of Mac. Evander and Mel were very interested in what Mac was doing with managing his deer herd. Mac was complaining there was no way of knowing how much good you were doing for the deer herd since it was so hard to see what the bucks looked like without spending all your time in the woods.

Mel, who was in the alarm business, had been telling Evander about the cameras they used in security situations that would take a picture when they sensed movement. Evander reasoned that such a camera would allow Mac to monitor his herd's development. Mac thought this to be a grand idea, and he had Mel order a couple of the cameras to check on his deer. Mac was hot to get the cameras since he was planning to go to New York to check out the Cortland County Deer Club's methods.

Meanwhile, Evander's deer lease was having the usual troubles hunting clubs experience. The problem was that he and Mel were doing all the work and the other guys in the lease were reaping the benefits. Every year, they posted the land, built the stands, and did all the paperwork that kept the lease alive. The other guys just showed up to hunt when the season arrived. Some didn't even arrive in time to help clean up the cabin.

One day in late summer, when they were at the lease looking around, Evander made a proposition to Mel. "If I can get the guys to really pitch in this year, will you cut up and package my deer?"

Knowing my uncle, Mel was suspicious. "How do you plan to do that?"

"I can make it happen if you'll order us one of those cameras," Evander shot back. "Will you do it?"

"Sure, I'd rather cut and package your deer than do all that other work. If you think you can swing it, I'll get you a camera and do what you say," Mel smiled.

As lease-posting day approached, Evander called everyone on the lease to inform them he was going to barbeque chicken. It was the best turn out for posting day in years. At lunch, Evander sent Bob Craft, one of the more slothful members, to Eckerd's to get the pictures in his deer camera developed so they could look at them while they ate lunch.

Bob came back grinning like a Cheshire cat. He was raving about the deer in the photos. The deer were huge with massive racks in velvet and lots of points and spread. It set the membership on fire. They decided to hang around after the posting was done to clean up around the shed where they skinned out the deer.

The whole nature of the deer club changed overnight. Every Saturday, guys were showing up to work. Stands were built; the cabin was spruced up; the guys even worked on the driveway in case it was rainy during the upcoming season. It was like a whole new deer club.

On opening day, Evander shot a nice, but not grand, 8 pointer. It was, however the biggest deer shot on opening day. He told Mel how he wanted it cut up and started back to the cabin to fix lunch. "Evander," Mel called before he got out of the shed. "How'd you do it? I know we didn't do enough to improve the deer at our lease. Why haven't we been seeing those huge bucks that were in the pictures? I won't be sore. I know you saved both of us a bunch of work, but how'd you do it?"

Evander smiled, "You know the pictures of the big bucks Bob got developed? I never said they were taken here; those deer are from the Cortland County Deer Club up in New York. I went up there with Mac for a visit and I put the camera out and took the pictures up there and brought the film down here to develop it! "

"Well," Mel grinned, "don't tell 'em any different. I'll cut up every deer you can shoot if you can keep these bums working. We might want to go to Yellowstone next year and get some pictures of elk."

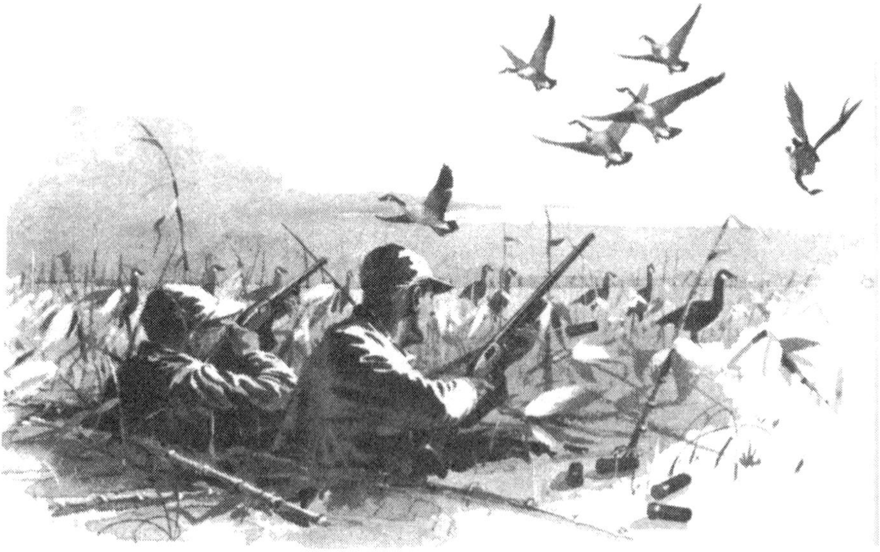

The Value of Optimism

John Anderson was always optimistic even under the worst circumstances. If we were duck hunting and it turned out to be a bluebird day, John would remind us that it was great weather and that the ducks might just fly anyway. If we were fishing, John always figured they were just getting ready to bite. On a particular day I'm thinking of, we planned to hunt a spot on the Yadkin River above the Bucks Steam Plant. Evander had gone into this little pond off the river and found it full of Yankee mallards, (ducks that had just come in from up north).

Since the ducks had just arrived, they wouldn't be as wary as they would be after every duck hunter from Burlington to Charlotte had tried to lure them into the standard two dozen mallard decoys that most duckers put out in those days. These ducks had been pushed down by a big cold front in Virginia and hadn't had time to be abused in North Carolina... yet.

The day started off perfect with the three of us getting breakfast at Evander's house and heading off by 4:00 a.m. John was pulling Evander's little

The Value of Optimism

duck boat with his huge Ford truck, and the three of us packed into the front seat, with me in the middle. By the time we got to the other side of Lexington, John noticed a vibration and asked Evander and me if we could feel it. How John noticed a vibration in the old Ford was amazing to me. I noticed about two dozen vibrations of varying frequencies and amplitudes. The Ford rattled, bumped, bounced, shimmied, and roared. It seemed that the tires must have been made of cast iron because it picked up every imperfection in the road surface and made it feel like a Pennsylvania pot hole.

A discussion began about how John could possibly detect another vibration, with Evander and me on the prosecution of the Ford and John handling defense. According to John, the Ford rode like a Bentley, and we were just looking for something to gripe about. Then the new vibration got strong enough for anyone to feel. We pulled off on the shoulder.

When we got out of the truck to check for the problem, it was instantly obvious that something was wrong with the trailer. It listed to the right unmistakably, and there was the smell of carbon in the air. When we got back to where the right tire was, or rather where the right tire was supposed to be, we could see the problem. We thought at first that the wheel had come off the hub. Once it was in the illumination of a flashlight, we saw that the wheel, or rather the center of the wheel, was still there.

Apparently, the tire had blown and eventually, or suddenly, had come off the rim. The wheel had run on the concrete surface of old Interstate 85 until it was just a disc slightly larger in diameter than

The Value of Optimism

the hub. It was red hot from the friction. John was unperturbed. We got back in the truck and trundled down the shoulder until we got to an exit, unhooked the boat, loaded all the stuff that might be stolen into the truck, and went back to Evander's house for another wheel and tire. John didn't even complain that Evander didn't have the spare on the boat trailer; he just seemed to think spare tires should be left at home instead of brought along on a trip.

By the time we got the new tire on the truck, it was time to have breakfast again, and we did. The whole time, John continued to be upbeat saying that now the boat ride wouldn't be as cold, that the eggs were cooked perfect, that the waitress had lost weight, and that the ducks would probably fly better in the middle of the day anyway. Outside, the sun shone bright and promised a bluebird day and no ducks. Evander was silent, mad at himself a little for not checking the tire closer and for not bringing the spare. I whined like a puppy saying that we might as well go home, the ducks wouldn't fly, there was no wind, it was going to be so bright we'd probably get sunburned, that I could have slept in, etc. We got to the spot at about 11:00 a.m. If I'd been driving, we'd have just gone home, but John was still enthusiastic.

It was one of the best days of duck hunting I've ever had. I sat on a log a few yards from the boat. It was comfortable, the silly Yankee mallards didn't know they weren't supposed to fly on bluebird days, and I got four mallard drakes. On the ride home in the shaking, grinding, noisy Ford, I was beaming. John took the opportunity to remind Evander and me how important it is to remain optimistic. I actually think it did have an effect on me. I was

The Value of Optimism

more optimistic for several months after that.

John lived near the drive-in theater and could see the movie from his front porch. That summer, Evander and I would sometimes go over to his house on Thursday night to see the movie for free. I could even hear it, though I had to repeat the critical parts since John and Evander's ears were desensitized from years of hearing guns going off. One night, the movie was a western about a cowboy who came home after being away for a long time. Rita Hayworth played his girlfriend. John was enthralled since he had a thing for Rita Hayworth. I had to repeat all her lines.

On Saturday night, Evander and I stopped by John's house to drop off a bushel basket of butterbeans. John was watching the movie again. On Tuesday, we were back to pick up some worm medicine for the dogs. John was watching the movie again. Evander joked at John and asked if he'd

The Value of Optimism

watched the movie every night. To our amazement, John replied that he had.

"John, I know you like Rita Hayworth, but you must have the movie memorized by now. Why are you watching it again?" Evander asked.

John looked over to us and smiled. "You remember the part when Rita Hayworth is about to take a bath on the porch of the cabin and the train comes?"

"Sure, I liked that part; she stopped undressing when she heard the whistle," Evander replied. "But you have that part memorized, too. Why keep watching the movie?"

John looked embarrassed, "One of these nights, that train's gonna be late."

As I said, John was always optimistic.

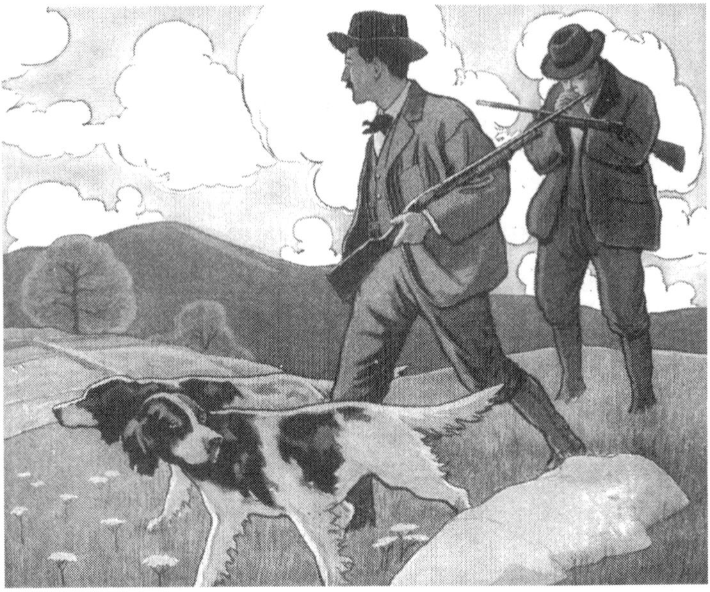

Merwin and Evander and the Bird Dogs Grave

Uncle Evander never met a stranger. We'd walk into a diner for lunch 300 miles from home, not knowing a soul within 25 miles, walk out with an invite for supper and wind up going hunting the next day on someone's farm when we didn't know him from Adam's house cat the day before. He just started talking to folks like he had known them all his life, and after they looked puzzled, because of trying to figure out who this guy was that obviously knew them, he would introduce himself. I suppose that a percentage thought he was a nut, and that was arguable, but they soon realized that he just liked people.

Sometimes, we never saw the folks we had dinner with again, and sometimes, they became part of the tremendous number of people who called Evander a friend. The fact was that he was the one who was plagued with trying to remember who people were, because they remembered him easier than he remembered them. After all, he had hordes of friends, and most people just don't make friends that easily.

I don't know where Evander met him, but one of his friends, Merwin Barrows, lived in Montana, and every couple of years Evander went out there to visit. Most, but not all, of Evander's friends had similar interests, and Merwin was no exception. Merwin was a bird hunter and bird hunting in Montana was as different from North Carolina hunting as a Pentecostal church service is from a Presbyterian one. The fact that it was so different made it especially interesting for Evander because he was always up for new adventure. To make things even more interesting, sometimes the two of them would head to Arizona to hunt Gambel's quail near Mayer.

Merwin had two dogs. Buck was as good a dog as a man could wish for and Jack was the kind of bird dog that Jack Nicholson would have been, had he been a dog. Evander was always frustrated when he hunted with Merwin because he was sure the hunt would have been a lot more productive if Jack had been left in the dog lot. Both dogs were short hairs, Buck being an old dog and Jack being younger, but old enough that he should have lost his puppy ways. Evander accused him of being a canine juvenile delinquent or at least suffering from some sort of arrested development.

Buck would point birds, and Jack would bust in and flush them before Merwin and Evander could get close enough for a shot. If they did get a shot, and got a bird, Jack would sneak off and flush up the singles while Buck was retrieving the dead birds. Jack had a fine nose, maybe better than that of his more respectable counterpart, but he seemed to delight in sabotaging what the other dog and the men were trying to accomplish. Merwin was certain that sooner or later Jack was going to make a world class dog; after all, he had potential. Evander was certain he'd never amount to anything, but he didn't want to hurt his friend's feelings.

One year, Evander and Merwin rendezvoused in Mayer for Gambel's quail and what is inevitable for all dogs, fine and sorry, had happened. Old Buck had died during the previous summer and left Merwin with Jack as his only dog. When Evander found this out, the level of distress he felt was considerable. Not only did he miss old Buck, all fine bird dogs are sorely missed when they go on to canine Valhalla, but he was stressed by the fact that he had driven over two thousand miles to spend the next few days of hunting in wonderful Gambel's quail country with the canine equivalent of a drunken rock star.

On the first morning, with Evander feeling considerable misgivings, Merwin, Evander, and Jack walked out into the hills that Merwin promised were swarming with birds. He'd probably have come out to visit Merwin if he'd known Buck was gone, but he would have had time to prepare himself for what he was sure he was about to experience. There is nothing in the world finer than hunting over a truly good dog and few things as frustrating as hunting over a boneheaded, high-strung mutt. Evander was sure they were in for a tough day and resolved to make the best of it. As Jack ranged across the draws, he mentally prepared himself to be gracious and not show his frustration to his host, who acted like they were in for the hunt of a lifetime.

Evander watched as Jack picked up the scent of birds, and anticipating a premature flush, he began to close ground between himself and the object of his frustration as fast as his old legs could carry him. Merwin noted that Jack was looking "birdy," but made no effort to rush in. Jack locked up in mid-stride, his body contorted by the fact that his front had managed to stop a millisecond before his rear, making him look like he'd slammed into some invisible barrier and had been frozen in motion. He was locked solid except for the fact that he was quivering at the rate of about 60 cycles per second. Although amazed that Jack had pointed the birds and not tried to run them off into the next county, Evander continued to walk fast until he realized that he was being impolite by rushing in to the point.

He forced himself to stop and wait until Merwin ambled over and caught up. Merwin walked in with Evander, the birds flushed, Jack relaxed a little, but held his place. Evander and Merwin each got a bird. Calmly, and with no visible surprise, Merwin cooed, "OK, fetch 'em up, Jack." And Jack brought back the two birds like he was a prize winning Lab.

They hunted across a couple more draws and Jack pointed again. This time Evander didn't rush as much, but he kept his gun ready in case Jack reverted to his old tricks. Merwin and Evander came up behind the dog and advanced across a little grassy section bordered by cat's paw and prickly pear.

"I think the birds have run," Merwin mumbled. "Jack, ease up on 'em." Jack looked cautiously at the men and advanced a few yards in full sneak. He moved as quiet as a church mouse, and after a few dozen yards, he locked up again. His eyes rolled back to the men to see if they'd noticed.

Merwin and Evander approached the dog again, and when the birds exploded, old Jack held steady as a rock. Again, he retrieved perfectly, bringing the birds to Merwin's hand and even dropping a bird in Merwin's coat pocket when he held the game bag open.

Evander took a long breath, rubbed his hand down his face and said, "Wow, Jack acts like a different dog now that Buck's gone. Do you think that somehow Buck made him nervous and that's the reason he used to act like such a bonehead?" Evander instantly regretted the choice of "bonehead" since Merwin had always acted like Jack was as good a dog as old Buck had been.

Merwin smiled and said, "No, I don't think that's it. You see, when old Buck died, I decided to bury him on the hill overlooking the house. He used to lie in the shade of that big pine in the summer and watch over the place. I dug the hole and I wasn't sure that it was big enough. You know how bad my back is, and I didn't want to put him in and have to lift him back out, so I made Jack get in it and lie down to be sure."

Evanders's eyes furrowed, "what does that have to do with it?"

Merwin grinned, "I think Jack got the idea that the grave was going to be for him, and he's been a great dog ever since!"

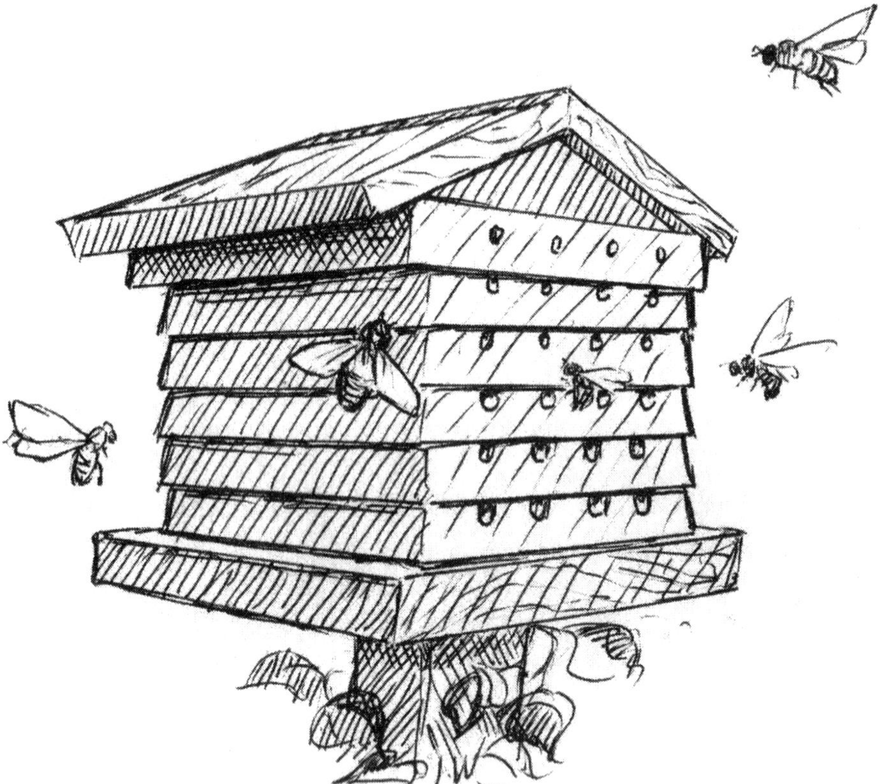

Miz Liza and Jimmy Beane

At fourteen years, young men often develop interests that change their whole outlook. I was affected as much as any young man, but for some reason, my friend, Jimmy Beane, got some sort of super injection of puberty. Jimmy developed a thin mustache and his voice changed, breaking in tone and varying from Steve Erkle to Barry White.

Jimmy's family was a whole lot different than mine, and for this reason I considered him to be much more worldly than I. His dad worked in a furniture plant and his mother a hoisery mill. His dad drove a '57 Ford convertible and his mom had a car, too. In our family, we only had one car and Mom didn't do public work. The Beanes didn't own the little house they lived in, they rented it from a friend of Evander's.

The whole family seemed strangely exotic to me, though I know I was naive in the ways of the world. Jimmy had an older brother who smoked and wore his hair in a ducktail. He wore tight jeans and cussed as much as anybody I knew, at least when their parents weren't around.

His mom and dad cussed a lot more than anyone in my family and his mom wore low cut dresses and a lot of makeup.

Jimmy was fascinated with the movies and movie stars, too. He would talk about Jane Mansfield, Marilyn Monroe, and Gina Lollobrigida for hours on end. The family went to the movies a lot and he was influenced by what he saw. He introduced me to smoking dried grape vines. They drew hard but you could draw smoke through them and smoke them like cigarettes. He also introduced me to rabbit tobacco. It's a stick like weed you can chew and it tastes a little like black pepper. I quit chewing it after Evander told me it tasted that way because male rabbits urinated on it to mark their territory.

Jimmy had a younger sister named Angela and she looked like her mother, dark haired and with dark eyes. They both reminded me of the Gypsy women I saw in the movies, exciting, but maybe a little scary. Angela made me nervous. She was only a couple of years younger than me but she somehow seemed to know she was wiser and superior to me in worldly issues. She was probably flirting with me, but I was too dumb to know it. I think puberty hit me a little later than Jimmy or maybe it hit me with a little less intensity.

Jimmy didn't go to school with me; he lived on Old Greensboro Road on one side of my favorite uncle, Evander Pritchert. I spent a lot of time at Uncle Evander's place during the summer and Jimmy and I fished, rode bikes to Hollis Motsinger's store for an occasional popsicle, and generally did the kinds of things boys do in the summer. Life was good and we had fun every summer. The summer we turned fourteen, we added discussions about girls to the activities and Jimmy was obsessed. He talked about girls at school, girls on TV shows, and girls in the movies, but mostly, he talked about Ms. Liza.

I'm aware that the title "Ms." became popular with the begining of the women's lib movement. It denoted a new title for women that didn't indicate their martial status. In the South, we discovered the Ms. term much earlier. In our case, it was more like Miz. It was an interchangeable term for any woman who was not our mama, our aunt, or some other female in our lives who was as close as family. Any woman who wasn't deeply involved in our lives received the title as a prefix to her first or last name.

Miz Liza was one of those women. Miz Liza lived on the other side of Uncle Evander and she was a peach. She was a naturally good looking woman with no pretensions. She was also interesting because she seemed to be our age at heart and she treated us like men. I'm sure she realized we were just kids who were turning into men, but she never acted like we were anything less than adults like her.

She was quite a bit older than us, but Jimmy didn't see that as a problem. She was also married to our friend, Harvey, who went fishing with us and fixed our bicycles, but that didn't stop Jimmy's fascination and fantasies either. Jimmy was constantly discussing what Miz Liza was wearing or how she smiled at him, and he didn't fail to mention her obvious feminine physical attributes.

You see, while Jimmy and I both had working knowledge of women's undergarments from our more than cursory attention to the women's foundations section of the Sears and Roebuck catalogue, Miz Liza didn't wear any foundational garments, not on top, at least. I think Jimmy would have been fascinated with Miz Liza anyway, but this certainly enhanced his attention.

One hot Saturday afternoon, Jimmy and I decided to ride our bikes to Harry Lee Hilton's pond for some fishing. Jimmy's bike had a low tire and we planned to stop by Miz Liza and Harvey's to pump the low tire on Harvey's air compressor.

Miz Liza kept bees, which always fascinated me. I couldn't imagine why anyone would cultivate something as evil as a honey bee, but to Miz Liza, they were just animals you kept around to make the plants grow better and furnish some honey. At one point, she'd explained that bees are just a part of nature, and provided you kept your wits and didn't do anything to arouse the bees, they weren't likely to sting you.

As we rode up, Miz Liza was briskly walking away from her hive. As we approached, she asked if one of us had a penny. I found one in my pocket and she took it and began rubbing her knuckle. She explained how she'd been checking on her bees when a guard bee stung her. She almost apologized for the bee, explaining how she'd not approached the hive the way she should've.

As she rubbed the penny on the sting, she explained how rubbing a sting with a penny would reduce the itching later. An expressioin of alarm came over her face. I heard the buzzing in her hair, and she rapidly reached around and pulled out the band that held her hair in a pony tail. Her long honey-colored hair fell around her head and

and shoulders as she shook it to free the bee. I glanced at Jimmy and saw that he had a look of unbridled lust in his eyes. To make matters worse, Miz Liza turned her head around so Jimmy could look to see if the bee was gone. He reached up and brushed his fingers though it and I saw his fingers tremble. His face was beet red.

Again we heard a buzzing and this time it was coming from inside Miz Liza's loose fitting cotton shirt. I saw real concern in her eyes but she remained calm. "Boys, I've got a bee in my shirt, and I'm going to have to take my shirt off. I want you to turn your heads."

I glanced at Jimmy and saw he was in a much agitated state. He took a ragged breath, looked at Miz Liza, and with his hoarse, pubescent voice, asked, "Which way?"

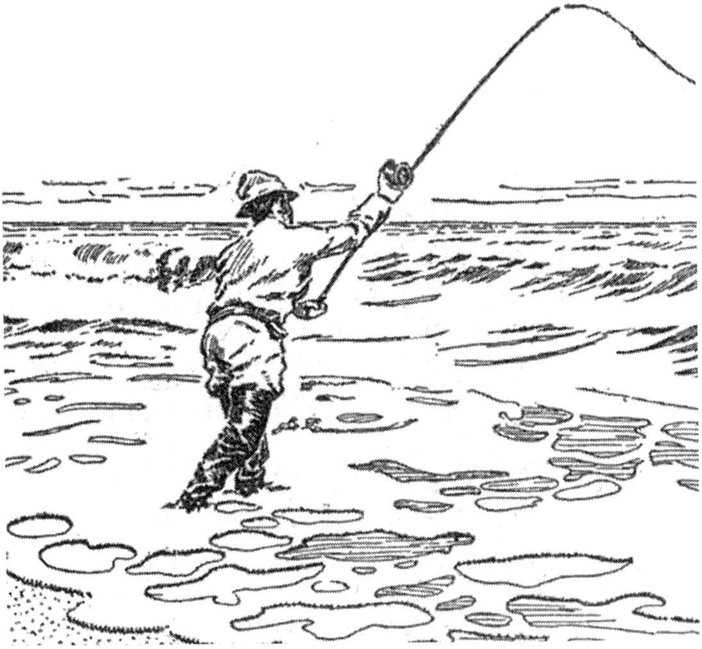

Nothing Like A Sure Thing

Evander and his friends loved a practical joke. The best kind of practical joke was luring the victim into making a bet that seemed ridiculous, and then smoking him with an inside plan. I remember sitting in Red Haymore's Wallburg Diner one day at lunch when Evander and one of his friends, Dave Motsinger, laughed 'till tears filled their eyes about a bet Dave had made the day before.

Dave Motsinger was one of Uncle Evander's best friends. They'd belonged to the same gun club for years, shot at the National Matches together, and even shot their first match together. Dave was a welder for RJ Reynolds Tobacco, and probably the most organized man I ever knew. He maintained and organized everything he owned, and could make anything with some metal and a welder. One reason for this was he had so much stuff, and it was organized so he could find it. His back yard was a series of sheds and buildings where he'd carefully stored all kinds of metal bars, rods and sheets, wire, pulleys, cables, motors, valves, boards, plywood, wheels, gears, photo frames, plumbing, and electrical equipment and absolutely everything else you could imagine a man could use. He did't just have it; he knew exactly where he had it stored.

At some point in Dave's shooting career, he got involved in shooting bowling pins off a steel table with a pistol. The winner of the match was determined by who cleared the table first, and Dave was pretty good at it. Dave, being the organizational addict he was, got involved and began to furnish the pins for the matches. He established a working relationship with a few bowling alleys and had a constant supply of pins for the matches. At some point, when he went to pick up bowling pins, the lady at the alley offered Dave a couple dozen old rental bowling balls. As I said, Dave's nature was never to turn down anything free. He took the balls and stored them in one of the organized sheds he had behind his house.

Tom Johnson was a bowler who worked with Dave, and he was the kind of bowler who lives, eats, sleeps, and dreams bowling. He bowled tournaments and leagues and practiced four times a week. You couldn't talk to him for two minutes without him referencing his bowling passion.

One day, he came to work telling about his new bowling ball. Dave had heard this routine before. According to Tom, every bowling lane required a different bowling ball. Supposedly, there was a difference in the wax and only an experienced bowler could determine which ball was the best to use. Dave assumed this was possible, but he was tired of hearing about bowling. As he was thinking this, Tom annouced that this new ball put him at owning twelve bowling balls, and he now had one to match every kind of lane.

Dave pounced. "I thought you were a real bowler. All you have is twelve bowling balls? Why, that's nothing. I hardly ever bowl, and I've got a lot more bowling balls than that." Dave stopped and waited for his victim to firmly grasp the bait.

Tom came back fast. "So how many bowling balls do you have?"

Dave knew he had his fish. "A man who knows how many bowling balls he has doesn't have many bowling balls," he said grandly. "I know I've got over two dozen."

Tom gowled, "You're a liar; you don't have two dozen bowling balls."

Dave's voice was level, calm, and had a legal tone to it. "I'll bet you ten dollars that tomorrow when I come to work, I'll have over two dozen bowling balls in the back of my truck."

Tom took the bet.

When Dave got home that night, he loaded about three dozen bowling balls in the truck. At break time, Dave and Tom and a party of interested onlookers walked out to Dave's truck. The official count was 39 bowling balls. Tom paid the bet, knew he'd been skunked and laughed it off. As they walked back to the plant, Tom asked, "Why did you load up 39 balls? All you needed to show me was two dozen."

Dave laughed, "Oh, I've got more than that. I just put enough in the truck so they wouldn't roll around on the way to work."

A practical joke/bet like this was considered to be an ultimate form of entertainment in Evander's circle of old men. It was a subtle plan, carefully executed and timed, and delivered complete satisfaction. It would be told and retold and I aspired

Nothing Like a Sure Thing

to learn the art.

Like Dave Motsinger, my Uncle Evander was never one to make a random bet. It was simply not his nature to leave anything to chance, so when he bet my Uncle Bernie that Billy Lagle would backlash his reel one day, I was amazed. True, Billy had been irritating everyone on the surf fishing trip bragging on how his new reel was backlash proof. Almost everyone else had experienced at least one backlash and Billy had laughed every time a reel blew up. He was out-casting everyone as well. Billy was a good caster, but he was really on his game on this particular trip.

As the truck jostled along the sandy beach, Evander puffed on his unlit cigar. "Bernie, Billy's really casting well this trip, but I'll bet he'll backlash today."

Bernie wasn't one to bet either, but Billy's casting had been so good that confidence pushed him over the limit. Besides that, Bernie was tired of Evander getting stuff off on him. "What are we betting, Evander?"

"Loser buys oysters at Pop's Raw Bar." Evander looked past me at Bernie, grinning through his cigar.

Within the first five minutes we were on the beach, Billy's reel blew up in the mother of all backlashes. Bernie had the look of a man who'd been beaten, but he didn't know how. We fished the morning bite and then hung around the point. About eleven, we headed off the beach and pulled into Pop's. Pop's is a tiny run-down restaurant/bar on the side of NC 12, just south of the main drag of Buxton, North Carolina. They have a plywood bar, a dart board, and some of the best scallops and oysters to be found anywhere. The oysters were as wonderful as always and Evander relished his. Bernie was suspicious, but he picked up Evander's tab. When they reached the register, the waitress told Bernie the tab was covered by a wealthy benefactor. Evander looked at me and winked; he'd paid the tab while Bernie was in the bathroom. Bernie was now even more confused.

Later at the fish cleaning station, Evander and I were alone, cleaning fish. As his protégé, Evander almost always let me in on his secrets, providing he wasn't scamming me. "How did you know Billy was going to backlash?" I asked.

"Hand me those Ziploc bags," Evander said. He always made me wait a minute before he revealed a trick. "Billy told me at breakfast he was going to replace his line and I told him he could put the line on my tab at Frank and Fran's if he'd backlash," Evander chuckled. "Hey, watch this," Evander said, carrying two fish heads to the edge of the grass. As Evander approached the brush, a raccoon came out and Evander tossed the fish head. Another came out and took the other fish head. Evander explained that the raccoons always hung around the fish cleaning table and would come running to get a free handout of fish every time they heard a door slam. He'd even named them Curley and Moe.

Over the next couple of days, I fished hard and thought even harder. I wanted to pull off a joke like the ones these old guys did, and it required a lot of thought to make it work properly. I had a lot to gain if I really did it and I didn't want to fail. I wanted to pull the joke on Uncle Evander, but I knew I couldn't because he'd figure it out and it wouldn't work. I decided on Uncle Bernie as the target.

Nothing Like a Sure Thing

On the way off the beach a couple of mornings later, I launched my plan as the truck again jostled across the sandy beach, coming back off the point. "Uncle Bernie, did you know you can call coons?" I asked in a conversational tone.

"What?" Bernie asked. "What are you talking about? I know you can sometimes get them to come to a predator call if that's what you mean."

"No, I can call them with my mouth; it sounds like this." I made a ridiculous clicking sound followed by a shrill whoop. "They come every time."

Bernie laughed. "Dick, you've been watching too many episodes of those Walt Disney nature shows."

I looked over at Evander and he had an approving but surreptitious smile.

"I'll bet you a pizza at Toppers I can call a coon up before we get back to Highway 12." We were only a mile or so away from NC 12. Toppers was the best pizza place on the island. It was also the only pizza place on the island, and the whole time we'd been there, we'd driven past it. Since Bernie was Italian, he figured a coastal islander in the South couldn't make pizza, so he had no interest in eating there. Evander had taken us to a lot of other places, but Toppers had been bypassed. I wanted pizza.

This conversation had taken us across the ramp, and we were within three hundred yards of the fish cleaning station. My timing had been impeccable. "Can we just pull off at the fish cleaning station? I can probably call a coon in from there." I smiled at Evander. Evander pulled into the little parking lot next to the fish cleaning table.

I was in the middle and I knew I had to act fast before Curley and Moe showed up. When Bernie opened the door to let me out, he was shaking his head as if to say Evander was crazy for encouraging such behavior. I started my calling before I even cleared the truck and started walking towards the scrubby bushes where the coons had appeared before. Curley and Moe were coming out of the grass as I approached, and I heard Bernie scoff behind me.

I opened the cooler on the front of the truck and took out two pieces of shrimp we had for bait. As I gave Curley and Moe their rewards, Larry showed up.

All the way to Toppers, Bernie raved about my ability to call coons. Evander smiled an approving smile, and I knew my stock had gone up more than a little that day. Bernie said the pizza was really good and gladly paid for it even after we let him in on the joke.

There are rites of passage for a young man. Some involve danger. Some involve love. Some involve sacrifice. This one might not have been as noble as the others, but at the end of the day, I knew I was closer to being an equal to these guys who were nice enough to spend some time with a skinny pimply-faced kid who'd just crossed a hurdle into their world of manhood. I swear I could tell a difference in the way Evander saw me after that, and he recounted the story with his friends with as much pride as if I was a young Masai warrior and had just killed my first lion.

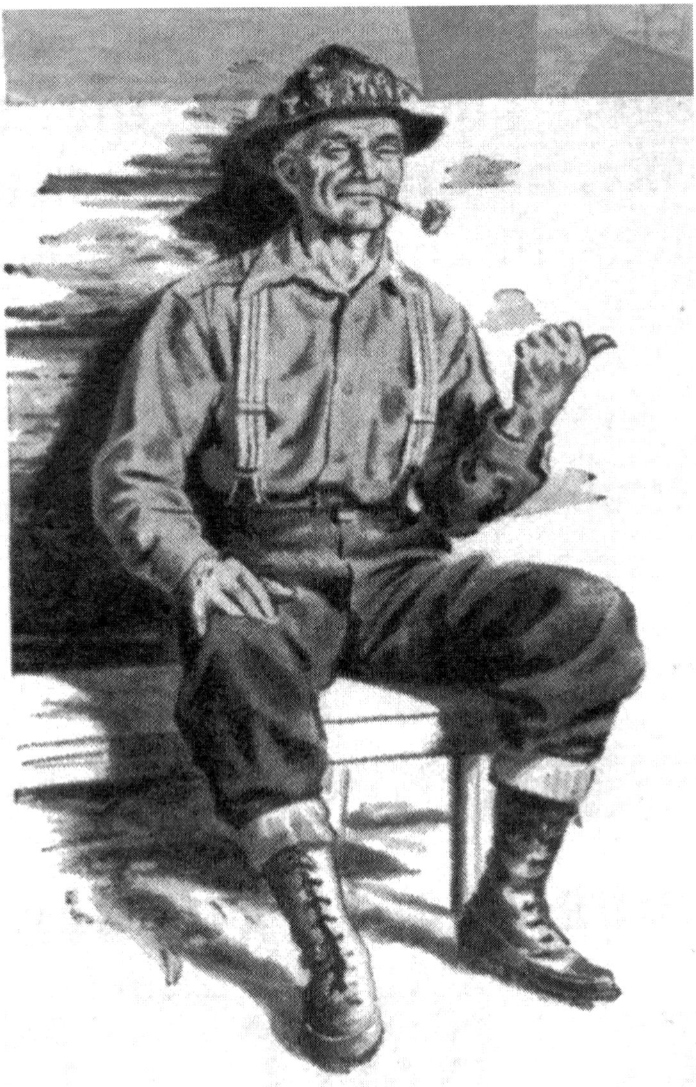

On Choosing Summer Attire

In Kermit Eller's yard there were two maple trees. They were just the right distance apart for their shade to overlap and provide a haven of coolness on a July afternoon. Kermit was a real farmer. Many of his contemporaries normally wore bib overalls every day of the week and had a new dark blue pair they wore on Sunday. Kermit didn't wear bib overalls, though. He wore bottle green Dickies work uniforms with long sleeves and a tee shirt underneath.

At almost 80, Kermit's face was dark from thousands of days in the sun. It was tracked with some lines caused by worries, I'm sure, but a lot of the lines were caused by smiles and laughter. When Kermit smiled, the smile covered his whole face, his thin lips moving back to reveal lots of tobacco-stained teeth. Kermit always had a chew in his mouth, and it's hard to keep pearly white teeth when you chew.

Kermit got up most mornings about 4:00 a.m. and had all his work done by 2:00 p.m. By 3:00 p.m. he would be in his hammock with a glass of Ethel's ice tea and his shepherd mix dog, Susie, lying underneath. He was not napping; he was awake and thinking; he was always happy to receive guests and offer a glass of ice tea.

Kermit was a slow talker. His brother, Frank, talked fast, but Kermit's slow talking made up for Frank's fast talking, and though they looked a lot alike, I could never imagine what thing (genetic or environment) caused the difference in speech patterns.

I don't remember what brought Jack Leonard and me over to Kermit's yard that day. Kermit had the best dove field in North Davidson County, and I often helped Kermit with mechanical issues as a way of compensating him for always making me welcome to shoot. Jack lived just a few hundred yards up the road from Kermit, and the two worked together on various projects like raising a field of potatoes or repairing a tractor. Within a few minutes, we had our glasses of tea, and Kermit was telling about Susie chasing a rabbit that had crossed right in front of the tractor that morning.

David Snider came walking down the road and angled off to the shade of Kermit's maples. He was sweating profusely and wearing the same kind of Dickies work clothes Kermit was wearing but without the tee shirt. It was hot. I was wearing a pair of shorts and a tee shirt and Jack was wearing shorts and a light cotton shirt.

David was a little older than I, a kind of unusual guy in that he seemed to be having a hard time finding himself. He seemed to imitate people he admired rather than be his own person. He was a hard worker, though, and he often helped Kermit when he needed help, like pulling tobacco or getting up hay. He'd just recently started wearing the Dickies, and I suspected he was wearing them because Kermit did.

David also had another characteristic. He would never back down from any position he started out on. Even if he realized he was wrong, he would never concede that he'd made a mistake. This was a little troublesome to Kermit since David would often spout some opinion about how something should be done before he found out what Kermit really wanted done, and then he'd argue with Kermit for a long time, trying to rescue the ill-fated idea.

Kermit was a thoughtful person and could present a good argument for his position, but he talked really slow, so he tended to waste a lot of time converting David over to his position. Eventually, David would strike on some angle he could use to allow him to do what Kermit wanted, but still be fundamentally right. While Kermit never complained, he just wasn't that kind of guy, it had to be frustrating for him and I sensed that he was trying to get David out of the habit.

While Kermit never seemed to sweat in his Dickies, David was sweating like an overworked mule. His face was red and rivulets of sweat rolled down his face and dripped off his chin. Jack remarked that maybe he'd be cooler in a short sleeve shirt and shorts. David had heard Kermit's defense of this clothing choice many times and repeated it, "If it will keep the heat in, it will keep the heat out," looking at Kermit to see if he noticed what he was saying.

I'd heard Kermit use that position many times and wondered if Kermit realized that he, himself, was generating 98.6 degrees of heat, about as warm as it gets in Davidson County. I would never have

On Choosing Summer Attire

challenged that response coming from Kermit since I considered him rightly as a wise man, but I decided to challenge the statement coming from David. "But David," I said, "you're generating 98 degrees of heat. Doesn't that mean the long sleeves are keeping you in 98 degrees?"

This had never occurred to David. He was not the brightest boy I knew; he looked to Kermit for a response. Kermit seemed to have not heard what I said. David was thinking. "The trick is to not exert yourself too much," he looked at Kermit again. "I never overexert myself; that's why I never run when it's hot."

Now, Kermit's ears perked up. He sensed an opportunity to work on David's habit of arguing his position to the last ditch. "I'll bet you do run when it's hot. Do you think it's hot today?" I saw a twinkle in Kermit's eyes and knew he was setting David up. "I'll bet you'll run before the day is out," Kermit snorted. The confidence in his statement was exaggerated to pull David in.

"What do you want to bet?" David asked, pleased to be in this as an equal with Kermit.

"If you run before the day's out, you have to help me and Frank get the hay up off his bottom for free." Kermit's eyes were merry. "And, if you don't, I'll take you to the Country Kitchen and buy you all the hot dogs, you can eat."

This was a serious bet. David Snider had once gotten into a wager with Windy Cecil that he could eat a dozen hotdogs all the way. He'd polished the hotdogs off without visible strain and ordered a big Pepsi later.

"You're on," David beamed and looked at us triumphantly, as if he had trapped Kermit into the wager.

A few minutes later, the sweaty David said he had to go and Kermit offered him a ride home on the fender of the tractor if he would hold the limbs out of his way while he bush-hogged under his apple tree. This sounded like a reasonable proposition except for the fact that Kermit never worked this time of day, and he would never have left his guests. He winked at Jack as David took up the offer.

We watched as the tractor rumbled the 200 yards or so to the tree and as David climbed down. Kermit put the tractor in high gear and took off. We could see the confusion on David's face, and then saw him swinging his arms wildly and running wide open behind the tractor as it bounced back toward us. David was just about to catch up with the tractor as Kermit pulled into the yard and shut it down. He was laughing so hard he could hardly get off and David ran up yelling, "Why didn't you tell me about the yellow jacket nest?"

Kermit chuckled and said, "Me and Frank are going to get that hay up Monday morning; have another glass of tea and we'll ride up to the Country Kitchen for a couple of hot dogs before I take you home."

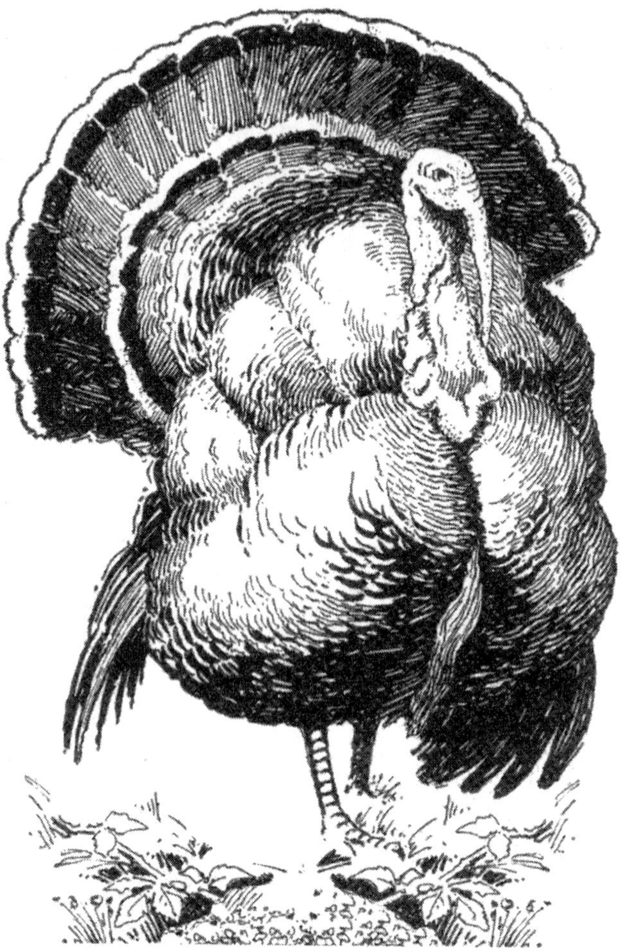

One Turkey is as Good as Another

If he could get there, Uncle Evander was in church on Sunday. My great-uncle was far from perfect, but he didn't miss many Sunday services. He was just as comfortable with the deacons as he was with the boys at Pop's Bar, and he saw both groups as having virtues and vices. He was always hospitable to the preachers, too. They often ate with him at home, and they hunted and fished with him.

A new pastor came to the church named Alvin Cox. Evander took a liking to Pastor Cox right away. I think what he liked about him was that he was not stuffy or dull like many of the preachers Evander had known. This fellow liked to fish and hunt and he liked to joke around. He smiled more than most preachers, and they got along right from the start.

He was different from my uncle in other ways, however, and Evander never quite understood them. Alvin made good money because the church was a pretty big one. He spent money on clothes and had a really nice house, but he was stingy with his money when it came to guns and tackle. To Evander this was next to blasphemy. My uncle made decent money, but if he had been poor as a pauper, he would have owned a nice shotgun. He couldn't stand a cheap fishing rod, either. If he had patches on his pants and he lived in a shack, he would have had good equipment. In a day when most people had Zebcos, my uncle had Ambassador 5000s. He appreciated fine shotguns and owned several A. H. Foxes and nice English double guns. He believed that shotguns and good tackle were the things that separated men of taste from people who lived their lives in some kind of darkness. He was not a snob. He would never discriminate against a man because he carried a Browning A5 or a model 12 Winchester, but he considered that man to be unenlightened.

He understood how the same fellow might feel that way about him because he didn't wear suits or have a college degree. He once told me, "We're all different; some of us can't imagine what it would be like to not live in New York City and not go to the theatre every weekend. They'd be miserable having to live the way I live and I'd be miserable to live like them. That doesn't make either of us wrong; it just makes us different." All that said, though, there was something that made him a little suspicious about a man who wasn't willing to sacrifice a little to own a fine gun.

Alvin Cox was one of those people, but the two of them were great friends anyway. When they fished together, Evander would try to encourage Alvin to upgrade his fishing equipment. It just irritated him to see someone fishing with cheap rods and Zebco reels. Alvin's response was always the same; "No one will know the difference a hundred years from now."

One day, Alvin came over to Evander's place

with the purpose of getting Evander's opinion on what kind of new shotgun he should buy. This was right up my uncle's alley. He loved to talk shotguns and was always flattered when someone asked him for advice about them. Evander didn't try to convince him to buy a gun like he used. He knew not everyone liked double triggers, and a lot of folks considered double barreled shotguns old-fashioned. He asked Alvin what he planned to do with the gun and made several suggestions, always trying to suggest a gun Alvin would get the most use out of that would last a lifetime. Alvin seemed too concerned about the cost of the gun and not concerned enough about the quality. Evander continually pushed towards spending more money and stressed that a valuable shotgun was an investment that would either last one's lifetime to be passed down, or if sold, bring enough money to justify the initial expense.

Alvin was tight when it came to guns as well as fishing equipment, though, and insisted the cheaper gun would serve his purpose just as well. When he came over to show my uncle his purchase, a cheap brand of over-under, he said, "I know I could have afforded a better gun, but nobody will know the difference a hundred years from now." My uncle said polite things about the gun, but wouldn't have been caught dead in a ditch with it.

The preacher wanted to try his new gun out, and being generous to a fault, Evander suggested they get his old Western Trap out of the shed and break a few clays. In those days, sporting clays had not been invented but my uncle's days on the rifle ranges had taught him the value of time behind the gun. He had a shed in a large field behind the house. There was power in the shed and an old Western clay trap on a small cart. Evander would often invite friends over for lunch on Sundays and they'd shoot clays from all sorts of angles to improve shooting skills. All his friends knew this and when they bought a new gun, or just wanted to shoot, they called and invited themselves to come and shoot. Evander saw this as a windfall since he loved to shoot, and it's not as much fun to do alone.

Evander picked up a gun and some shells and they walked out to the shed. They rolled the trap out, loaded it with targets, and proceeded to shoot. On the first shotgun report, there was the loud unmistakable gobble of a tom turkey. This was a warm February day and Evander immediately recognized the sound as being old Tom. Tom was Evander's neighbor's turkey and the largest specimen of a turkey I ever saw. Tom's owner, Lincoln Taylor, said Tom weighed 45 pounds, and I believed it, too. Tom was as amorous as he was obese and would strut up to anything from a dog to a boat on a trailer. He gobbled at any loud sound and was so fat he would be exhausted from walking across Lincoln's yard.

The preacher heard the gobble, too, and he looked at Evander in amazement. "Was that a turkey?"

My uncle responded, "Sure, this place is lousy with 'em. You want to turkey hunt when the season comes in?"

The preacher was overjoyed. "I'd love to!" My uncle grinned and told Alvin that nothing would please him more, and with that, plans were made.

Alvin had never hunted turkeys before and his excitement boiled over. Every Sunday he'd mention the event. One Sunday he even mentioned it from the pulpit. He asked Evander what kind of

One Turkey is as Good as Another

clothes he needed, and Evander advised him on what to buy. Evander also counseled him to buy several kinds of shotgun shells and pattern his gun to find which gave the best results. By the time the season rolled around, the preacher had read books on turkey hunting, patterned his shotgun, talked to everyone he knew who was a turkey hunter, and bought a complete set of camouflage clothes. He was prepared.

Uncle Evander invited him over for breakfast the morning of the hunt. Alvin arrived at 5:00AM as Evander was setting the table with a huge breakfast of eggs, bacon, grits, fried potatoes, biscuits, and hot coffee. While they ate, Evander expounded on the importance of being quiet in the woods and warned Alvin that turkeys have very sharp eyes. When they'd finished eating, Evander told the preacher to put on his hat and let him see what he looked like in it. My uncle gazed at him in concern.

"I'm afraid the turkeys will see your face, Alvin. We're going to have to fix that." He took a piece of blackened wood out of the fireplace and crumbled it up. He smeared the soot on the preacher's face and carefully covered up the pale features until Alvin's face was as black as the gates of hell. "That's better," he said. "Let's get going."

Evander led and Pastor Alvin followed as they traversed the cow pasture and crossed the creek in the pre-dawn darkness. They hid themselves in the honeysuckle and Evander pulled on an old box call and made a few quiet clucks. There was no response. They sat there a few more minutes, and Evander clucked a few more times. Still no response. Evander whispered, "Let's try another spot." Alvin nodded in agreement and followed my uncle as he trudged through the swamp along the creek a half mile. Once again, they backed into a thicket and Evander made a few clucks. There were all kinds of forest sounds, but there were no turkey sounds. A few minutes later my uncle repeated the drill with the same results.

"I know a spot that will surely work," Evander whispered, and once again they slogged through the muck and woods in a long winding route that brought them within a quarter mile of where they'd started. Evander told Alvin that he was going to try a shock call to try and locate a gobbler. He made a noise that sounded just like an owl with love on his mind. The preacher was amazed at how realistic the sound was. It was almost startling. This time there was an answer... the strong, unmistakable gobble of a turkey.

Evander whispered instructions to the preacher on the importance of a quiet move and told him that they would move to a good position and set up to call the gobbler in. They crept forward at a snail's pace for two hundred yards, and Evander motioned to the preacher to hide. He made a couple of clucks and was rewarded with a loud, startling gobble. It sounded very close. "Get ready," he whispered. They waited a few minutes and he clucked again. The return was instant, the gobble strong and fierce, but the turkey seemed to be in the same place. After another wait Evander whispered that they'd have to move around a little to get the turkey to come in from another angle since he had to cross a little stream to come straight to them. Alvin nodded again and they moved as slow as syrup through some of the thickest tangles the dark-faced preacher had ever seen.

It took a half an hour to cover a hundred yards and Alvin's heart was pounding like a jackhammer the whole time. He felt the perspiration streaming down his face in rivulets and worried that the blacking was running off. Knowing the turkey was so close, and they had a good chance at him if they just could get a little further without spooking him was almost more than he could bear. Eventually, they came to what looked like a clearing where he made out the shape of the largest turkey, or bird of any kind for that matter, that he had ever seen. "Shoot him!" Evander whispered in a loud stage whisper.

Alvin noticed the honeycomb pattern of chicken wire between them and as his eyes adjusted to the light, he saw the turkey was the color of dirty snow. He protested, "But he's a tame turkey in a lot!"

Evander smiled, "Go ahead Preacher. Nobody'll know the difference a hundred years from now."

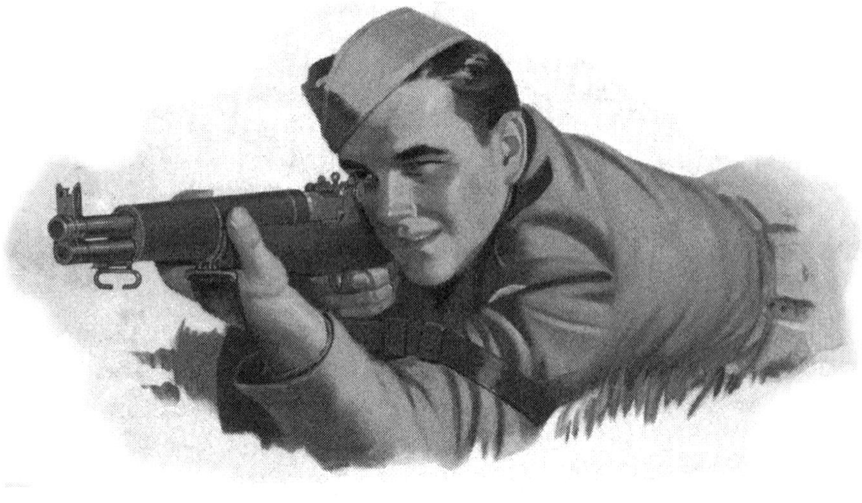

Russell Jones and the UFO Sighting

My Uncle, Evander Pritchert, was a naturally picky man who made a resolution at some time in life not to be that way. As a result, I think he led a conflicted life, internally organized and even anal about things, but outwardly accepting of things as they happened. One of his heroes was Teddy Roosevelt, a man who began life as a sickly child but determined himself to be tough. As a young man, Teddy looked like a book worm and subjected himself to the toughest life he could find in the American West. Evander was kind of that way about his own fastidiousness.

Russell Jones was a quiet guy who began competing in High Power Rifle competition about the same time as Uncle Evander. High Power shooters tended to pair up, since matches were shot with two men on the line and two in the pits working targets. When one shooter was shooting, the other was scoring him, and when their turn came, they worked together in the pits. Since a weekend match would consist of spending at least 16 hours together, one chose one's shooting partner carefully. Evander and Russell both started with other shooting partners, but like divorcees, both wound up without a partner.

Russell was the best shooting partner a guy could have. He was a good shooter, really a better shooter than Evander. He was calm and relaxed, which balanced Evander's intense nature nicely. Russell was an easygoing, though sometimes slow to get started, traveler, and he was fair and honest. All this being said, no one ever wanted to share a room with Russell.

Russell had a snoring problem. In fact, to say Russell had a snoring problem was like saying Lindsay Lohan has behavior problems. Russell snored like no man Evander had ever heard. He was capable of both high and low pitched snores, his cadence tended to change on a regular basis, and the snoring began predictably as soon as Russell fell asleep. The hutments used at Camp Perry in those days were 14 foot square buildings with a six foot space between each one. It was common for people three huts away (60 feet and six walls away) to complain when Russell had a louder than normal night.

When Russell and Evander began pairing up for matches, Evander knew this meant he'd be spending time sleeping in the same room as Russell, but Russell was such a great guy and shooting partner, he was willing to accept the challenge. He suspected the reluctance of other shooters to share a motel room or hut at Camp Perry had bothered Russell at some point, but he figured he was enough of a man to rise above such self-centered pettiness and planned to demonstrate this to those who'd discriminated against Russell because of his night singing.

Evander was the kind of guy who believed in will. He demonstrated this by simply falling asleep before Russell most nights, and willing himself not to wake up during the cacophony of snores that Russell generated while his raveled sleeve of care was being re-knit by sleep. It worked remarkably well during regular weekend shooting events, but the National Trophy Matches lasted a week and the more tired Russ was, the quicker he went to sleep, and the louder he snored. Their first week-long trip in a Camp Perry hut resulted in some lost sleep for Evander, but overall it was manageable.

The second year they bunked together, they stayed for both the Trophy Matches and the Championships and shared a hut for 16 days. By the time the trip was over, Evander was suffering from mild sleep deprivation, but managing fairly well. He did, on a couple of occasions, wake Russell and tell him he was snoring, which probably was curious to Russell because he knew he snored as well as anyone else who'd tried to sleep within the above-mentioned 60 feet. He snored so loud, he sometimes woke himself up. Apparently, this mention of snoring as if it normally didn't happen confused him because he didn't go back to sleep instantly, allowing Evander to beat him to sleep and get through the rest of the night.

Evander was methodical in nature and loved to work through a problem. As soon as they were home, he began thinking of how he would work through this one. Plugging his ears didn't help; he just couldn't sleep this way. He didn't like waking Russell to tell him the snoring was bothering him. In the traditional Southern mindset, Evander thought his friend had as much right to a good night's sleep as he did, and it would be rude to wake him and tell him he was snoring every time it just happened to bother him.

One day, he was in a store and noticed a toy he saw use for. The toy looked like a tiny spaceship, had flashing lights, and made spaceship sounds. It had a little loop on the top, and Evander bought it, knowing it would be good for at least one night's sleep. He tied a length of fishing line on it and put it in his stuff that went with him to Camp Perry.

A few nights into the Championships the snoring was so loud, it woke Evander up. He tried to simply go back to sleep, but it was impossible. He quietly opened his bag and removed the space ship. He looped the line on his cleaning rod and turned on the lights and sound. In the darkness of the little hut, the space ship looked like something out of a low budget science fiction movie. Russell was making sounds like a bellowing bull fighting a cougar as the spaceship began a slow decent over his face. In the dim hut, the flashing lights cast an eerie glow over Russell's peaceful countenance.

Evander was sitting up on his bed as he lowered the ship and it was just over Russell's nose when he woke enough to recognize the intrusion. He snorted and scrunched down into the already sagging World War II Army cot as Evander swung the light back and turned off the switch that controlled the lights and sound. Quietly, he lay back in his bed, listening to Russell's uneven breathing.

As he lay there in the dark, he wondered if he'd gone too far. He also wondered if restraining his laughter would keep him from beating Russell back to sleep, but he managed to drop off before the snoring started again, and if it did, he was sleeping too well to hear it.

He only had to repeat the spaceship trick once more during the whole two weeks; maybe Russell was taking longer to go to sleep, maybe he wasn't snoring as loud or maybe, Evander considered, the spaceship was inhibiting his sleep.

By the time the two weeks were over, he felt a little guilty about the trick. He decided to ask Russell if he'd been sleeping well; he certainly had shot well. "Have you been sleeping OK?" he asked on the next to the last day.

"I've been sleeping fine," Russell said slowly, "but I'm dreaming about spaceships a lot."

"It's probably all the restaurant food we've been eating," he answered.

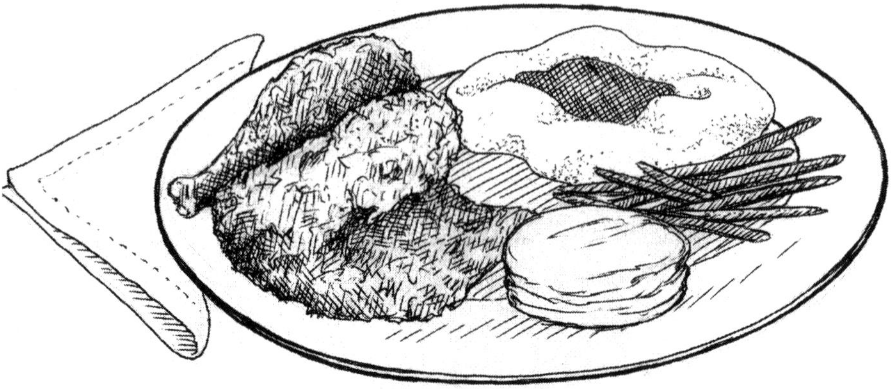

Say the Blessing, Bob

Recently, I walked through the house during the Martha Stewart show. Martha was extolling the virtues of the Farm Hand granola bar. It seems some enterprising lady came up with a new granola bar, and Martha was showcasing her product and entrepreneurial skills. Having spent the early years of my life as a farm hand, I can assure you that no real farm hand would get excited about a granola bar. I've tried granola bars, and they're ok (if you like that sort of thing) but not sufficient fuel to keep a real farm hand going.

The one thing that made working in the fields worthwhile was dinner. No, I don't mean supper, I mean dinner. Dinner was served around noon in those days and comprised the main meal of the day. For bailing hay, chopping wood, killing hogs, planting, hoeing, topping, or pulling "backer," the meal was an event that almost made the whole miserable endeavor worthwhile. As a kid, my preference for spending a day out of school was fishing or hunting. There was no farmer gene in my DNA. I like the fried okra, the cornfield beans, the home grown tomatoes, and the watermelons, but I just don't get a kick out of working dirt. This may have come from my being abused by Mama in that accursed dahlia patch she had. I'm sure that, had she abused me in modern times, I would have shown up on 60 Minutes and made national news for child abuse.

Farm hand meals when I was a kid consisted of probably two kinds of meat. Country style steak, meatloaf, fried chicken, tenderloin, or roast beef were the normal fare. The space on the table around these was occupied by lots of vegetables. Everything was likely grown on the farm or swapped from a neighbor. Most of the time it was fresh. When it was canned, it was canned in a glass jar and put up in the summer by Mama, Grandmother, or Aunt Dinky. Almost every meal included pinto beans and some form of potatoes. All meals were accompanied by homemade light rolls or biscuits. There was no square white bread on the table and no round canned biscuits. This just didn't happen. That was for city people. The closest we ever got to a granola bar was oatmeal cookies and the Micky's snack cakes that Uncle Bill bought at the day-old bread store. I'm not complaining; they were good, especially at 9:00 break in a dew covered tobacco field.

When we came in from the field, the table would be covered with dishes and have barely enough room around the edges for plates. Sometimes, once your plate was loaded up, there was room to eat at the table but normally, we kids ate on the front porch or back porch steps with our plates on our knees. Of course, before any taking out of dishes began, somebody said a blessing. It might be the youngest of the cousins, and it might be Granddad, but someone said a blessing. While all this agricultural work was being done, my Uncle Evander was somewhere fishing, working a dog, or perhaps, in the right season, hunting. He would cut wood, cut up hogs, or help get up hay, but he had a serious aversion to dirt, fertilizer, and plants.

I haven't attended a feast like that in years; sure, I see plenty of food on tables, but there was something about those work dinners that made for the best eating of my life. The funny thing was that eating those big dinners didn't make me sleepy like a big Thanksgiving dinner does now. I guess we didn't have time to get sleepy since we went right back to the field.

I sat down to the table with plenty of big spreads when I was running with Evander, though the circumstances and fare were often different. Those meals consisted of the same vegetables most of the time but not so many varieties on the table at one time. The main course would be catfish, striper, venison, doves and gravy, fried quail, or country style ducks. Sometimes there would be shrimp, oyster or salmon stew. Most of Evander's friends liked his cooking, but some were pretty good cooks on their own. Bob Craft was one of them, and Bob prided himself on having everything ready within the same minute. The butterbeans would be turned off, the stewed potatoes would be ready, and the fried striper fillets would come out of the grease within the same 30 seconds or so that the biscuits came out of the oven. Everything went to the table so hot you couldn't cheat and eat a bite before the blessing. You could get a third degree burn off one of those biscuits.

Bob was somewhat long-winded when it

Say the Blessing, Bob

came to saying the blessing. He would be grateful for the sunrise, for the fish we did or didn't catch, for all his friends, for the way the boat motor ran and then he would cover prayer concerns. I was often hungry and sometimes a little frustrated with listening to Bob's booming voice drone on about someone's goiter while my mouth watered. It wasn't that I wasn't grateful, I just figured God had created all this and had things pretty much in hand and that Bob's contributions weren't going to provide any new ideas.

I noticed that Evander got a little restless during Bob's pre-meal prayer time, too. When Bob was present at Evander's or someone else's house, as soon as we were ready to eat, Evander would announce that he wanted to say the blessing or maybe give me the assignment. If Bob wasn't present, he would defer the duty to someone else. I also noticed that, when we were eating at Bob's house, Evander would not jump in with the blessing. In fact, he would often ask Bob to say it. One evening, as we left Bob's house in the old, green truck going back to the little shack we stayed in when we were down at Bob's place, in Tyrell County, I asked him about it.

"I've noticed that most of the time when Bob eats with us you say the blessing or have me to say it," I asked. "Why do you do that?"

"Haven't you noticed how long Bob's blessings are?" Evander came back, "I just do that to save time."

"How come you always let Bob pray when we eat at his house?"

"Well, a man is the king of his domain," Evander began, blowing a cloud of smoke out of his cigar. It promptly disappeared out the narrow crack in the side window. "Where you live, you're in charge of everything. He is the king of his house. It would be presumptuous of me to say the blessing over his food at his house without his asking me to."

He looked at me and winked. "Besides, we have to do something while we wait for the food to cool off."

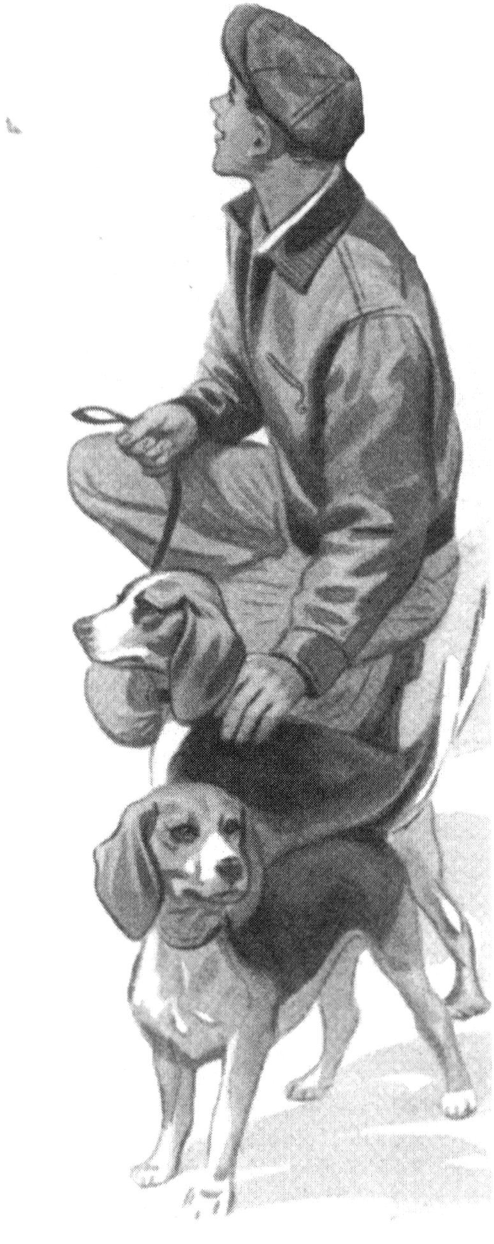

Sometimes It's Better to be Wrong

My uncle was in a molting stage. Well, he wasn't really molting, but he had that kind of ruffled appearance of a molting bird. It was October, and therefore time for the wardrobe change that occurred twice a year for him.

Evander was not vain by most men's standards. He did not own a nice suit. He did get his shirts laundered, though, and normally they were crisp and starched. For the two weeks or so in his transitional period, his shirts were wrinkled.

At some point in October and later in May, he would put the freshly laundered shirts that were out of season in the wooden box under his bed and bring out the upcoming season's shirts, wrinkled from six months in the box. He wore wrinkled shirts until he was through the cycle and all the new season's shirts had been laundered.

He did this with his pants as well, but these didn't show the wrinkles like the shirts. He only got his shirts laundered. I've never figured out what motivated this otherwise unkempt man to spend money getting his shirts laundered. I suspected at one time, it had something to do with the pretty Korean lady at the desk of the laundry, but he continued to get the shirts washed and pressed after she left and was replaced by an old Korean guy with a white beard.

On this particular visit, his outward reason for stopping by our house was to check to see if I'd wormed the beagles. His inward reason was that Mama had just made persimmon pudding. The beagles didn't belong to either Evander or me. They belonged to my cousin, Buck, who was, at that time, in Alaska with the Army. He asked me as we watched the dogs romp in the lot if I had given them the worm medicine. "Yes, sir," was my prompt answer, but I was chastising my self for forgetting. I figured that as soon as he left I'd do it, and no one would be the wiser.

"Are you sure?" he asked. "Ain't that the worm pills right there?" He pointed to the shelf on the wall of the old hog house where we kept the dog supplies. I was busted.

"Somebody must have bought another batch. I'm sure I already did it," I lied. I knew that it was a flimsy cover-up but I stuck to my guns. "I'm sure I did."

He was quiet for a moment. "Do you think you might be mistaken?" He then let the silence do its work.

"I might have been wrong," I admitted. We wormed the beagles.

A few weeks later, in his old, green Chevy truck, I admitted to him that I'd lied about worming the dogs. We were driving down to Bob Craft's farm, near the Alligator River, to hunt birds. "There's nothing bad about admitting you're wrong," he said.

Sometimes It's Better to be Wrong

"When you do it, you gain credibility with most folks." I couldn't understand how that could be.

He patiently explained how most people refuse to admit they're wrong, and how when you admit you're wrong, people realize you're being honest and that gains their trust. "Besides, sometimes being wrong pays off. I'll show you how later," he said and winked. I knew him too well to try to get him to tell me what he meant. I knew I had to wait.

When we got to Bob's, we went through all the conversation that comes with being from the South and meeting someone you haven't seen in a while. That took a few minutes. Evander and Bob eventually got around to talking birds and dogs. Young dogs were discussed and plans for tomorrow's bird hunt were made. We had a supper of fried quail with gravy, turnip greens, and grits.

After supper, I looked at gun catalogs that were in the living room of the old hunting house, and they smoked cigars and told stories. They were still talking when I went off to bed.

When morning came, I was hot to go. They ate a leisurely breakfast, drank coffee, and told more stories. I champed at the bit. Evander advised me there was no use tramping over ground looking for birds until most of the frost had melted off. I knew he was right, but I complained anyway.

The plan was to hunt until a little after lunch time and then go into Columbia to eat lunch at Flossie's. Flossie's was a "meat and three" place that had fresh fish on Fridays, and fresh fish in Columbia meant that it was swimming that morning. For those not raised in that part of the country, "meat and three" means the meat of your choice and three vegetables from a lineup of ten or so. Most "meat and three" places are nothing to brag about, but Flossie's was exceptional. Her vegetables were real, not from a can, and my favorite was cucumbers and onions in vinegar and water.

I don't remember exactly where we hunted. I know it was a wonderful fall day in Eastern North Carolina because now I remember the fall sunshine more than how we got to the fields. If you've been to Eastern North Carolina during the early part of bird season, then I've said enough. It is the finest place I know of for that time of year. All the things that make Tyrell County miserable in summer are dead or dormant in bird season. Sure, a few cockleburs and beggar lice are still around, but that's a small distraction.

I do remember that after the hunt was over, I was tired. Evander carried his little 20 gauge Fox, and Bob had a little Charles Daly over/under. I was hunting with my Ted Williams 20 gauge automatic with a vent rib and adjustable choke. I'd bought it with money earned by pulling tobacco, and therefore, had paid in sweat and blood.

I'd decided, based on the ramblings of numerous gun writers, that the perfect gun for the modern man was a semi automatic, three inch magnum, 20 gauge. Truly a versatile gun, it could be used for bird hunting or duck hunting. I just didn't realize at the time that it wasn't very good for either.

Ted Williams must have been one heck of an athlete. He would have had to be tough to carry his seven-pounds-plus creation on a quail hunt. I don't know what happened to that gun. My mind must have mercifully blocked out the memory. I didn't shoot well, though, and if I remember right,

Sometimes It's Better to be Wrong

the dogs didn't turn in their best performance. Still, we managed to bring in fourteen birds between the three of us.

Sitting at the table at Flossie's, Bob remarked that in spite of the poor take, it was an enjoyable hunt. Evander spoke up. "Sixteen birds is not such a bad bag for the conditions and the way the dogs worked."

Bob corrected him, "Fourteen birds."

Evander seemed surprised. "There were sixteen birds, Bob. Your mind is slipping," Evander said, flatly. I stayed quiet. I thought that Evander must have been tired to miscount the birds as he normally was sharp to the point of frustration to normal people.

Bob took a deep breath and said, "Evander, you saw the birds and counted them yourself; you know there were fourteen."

Evander came back, "You think I'm wrong. I say there are sixteen birds. We'll go out to the truck and count 'em. Will you buy my lunch if I'm wrong?"

Bob sensed that Evander was at the end of his rope. "Yes, I will!" he said with triumph in his eye.

Evander winked at me and said, "You know, we can go out there and count the birds, but now that I think about it, I believe I'm wrong. And I appreciate you buying my lunch. See, Dick, sometimes it is better to be wrong."

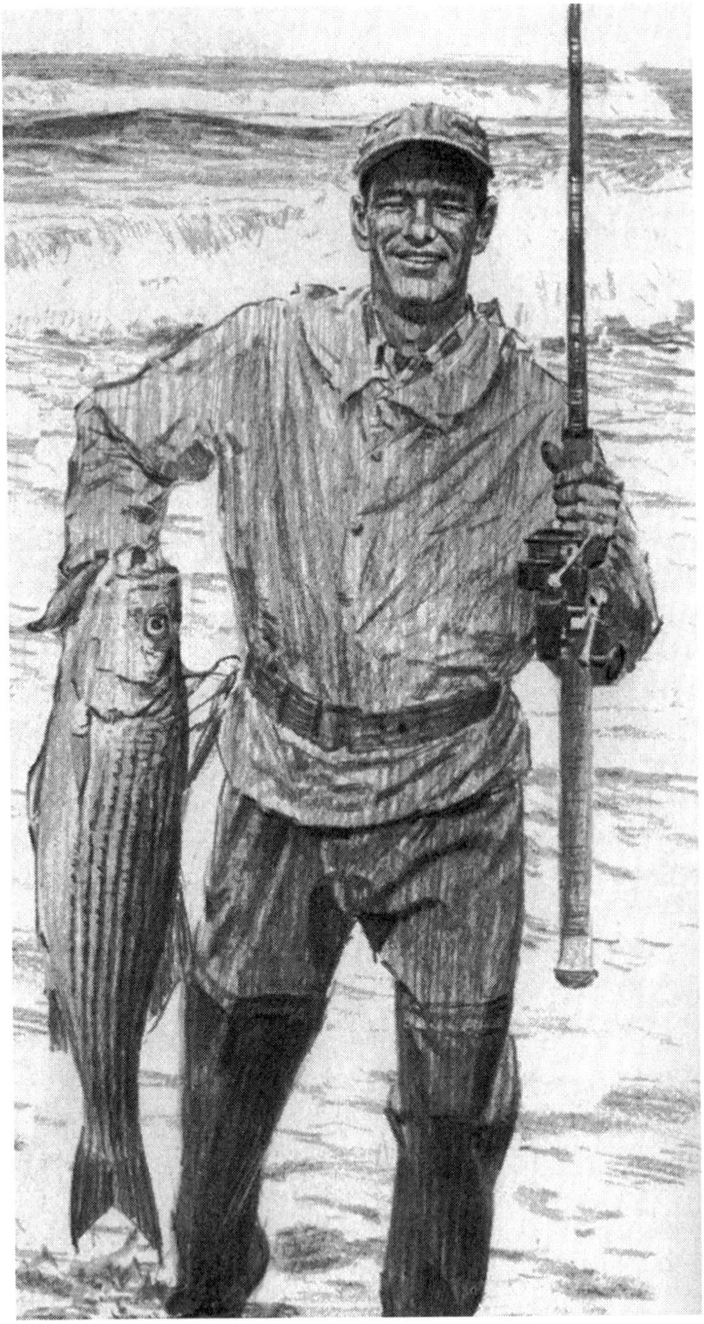

Striper Run for Stumpy

Evander Pritchert loved to be alone. Anyone could see this from the way he lived. He told me once that when he was alone he was happiest because it allowed him to think. He was happiest alone, but he would take anybody hunting or fishing who would go with him. I asked him about this because it didn't make sense to me. "God has blessed me with so much I just can't bear to live with myself if I don't share," he muttered. I've watched him wince as he allowed people with less experience backlash his reels, break his rods, slam his fine shotguns closed like someone slamming a dump truck door and undo months of training with his bird dogs. I never saw him blow his top.

He'd suggest the greenhorn keep his thumb over the spool or perhaps this spinning rod would work as well. Or maybe he'd patiently explain how a 90-year-old shotgun should be closed gently since it will function just as well closed gently as it will when slammed. I've seen him come home and re-spool the reels the person he invited to go fishing with him used because the line on them was hopelessly twisted. If you threw away a plug that cost three dollars, he'd pull another one out of the tackle box and tie it on for you to snag on the bottom and break off.

He loved to fish and hunt with just him and old Bob, his Lab, but his conscience would not allow him to go alone when someone else could enjoy the trip. In fact, he invited all kinds of people who told him they wanted to go somewhere with him, and when he invited them, they often turned him down. They always had something to do. He never stopped asking, though. He never met a kid that he didn't want to take fishing, or an old person for that matter. I think he felt as if he was an ambassador to the outdoors, and his job was to make everyone he knew fall in love with being outside.

He was that way with Stumpy Conway. Stumpy was a nice guy. He just hadn't had a lot of great experiences outdoors and I think Evander wanted to make up for that. Stumpy would come over and shoot, and Evander would pull targets for him till the cows came home and never seem to notice he didn't ever bring the box of clays he kept talking about bringing to replace the ones he shot. A lot of people came over to Evander's and shot clay targets, and most of them more than made up for it. Some would take him out to dinner, some gave him a ham at Christmas; some took him on trips and paid his way. He thought that was the way it should be. He would tell me about how Doc Fletcher had invited him to shoot birds in Georgia, and though he enjoyed the trip, he was most proud that his friend was considerate and thoughtful.

In Evander's opinion, two words to describe a real sportsman were: considerate and thoughtful.

If you were hunting with a friend and he ran out of shells, you shared with him so you both ran out at the same time. If someone at the boat landing had a flat tire, a true sportsman would spend part of his fishing time to help him get squared away. That was just the way it was. If something came up that you couldn't duck hunt with someone next week, you called and told him and apologized as soon as you found out. That way he could make plans and find another shooting partner so as not to ruin his trip.

Stumpy envied the results Evander got in the field, and that was obvious. Evander gave tips and advice, but somehow Stumpy's efforts didn't pay off the way they should. He just seemed to be unlucky.

Evander had found a little river in the Foothills of North Carolina that was thick with wood ducks in the early season. He'd float this little river in an Old Town canoe with a homemade blind on the front and always get good shooting. He even killed some mallards on that river. His good results came as a result of hard work because he would scout the different sections of the river in September to find where the ducks were using. He didn't see paddling twelve miles of river as work, though, because to him it was just part of the hunting process.

Evander decided to take Stumpy with him on the Johns River on opening day. He figured floating the river was a way to always get ducks, and if he showed Stumpy how to do it, he would have furnished him with a reliable and almost foolproof method of waterfowling. Stumpy was overjoyed and told his friends that he and Evander were going to hunt together.

The plan was that the two of them would meet at the Highway 18 bridge on the Johns River at

4:00 a.m. This would allow them to leave Stumpy's truck at that boat landing and then drive up to Corpening Bridge in Evander's old Chevy pickup. They would then put the boat in the water, float the river and have Stumpy's truck at the takeout point to allow them to go back to Corpening Bridge to get Evander's Chevy. The drive up to the Johns was about two hours, so it involved a very early start. Evander talked to Stumpy a couple of nights before to explain how he was staying in Hickory at a friend's house and gave Stumpy the number so he could call in case something happened. "Don't worry, I'll be there," Stumpy said.

On opening morning, Evander was sitting in the gravel parking lot at 3:45 a.m. At 4:30 there was still no Stumpy. He figured Stumpy had truck trouble and figured that the day was not wasted yet. He'd allowed for problems and had planned on being at the put-in point at Corpening Bridge almost an hour ahead of time. He fell asleep in the truck. At 5:30, he saw headlights and got out of the truck in anticipation of loading Stumpy's stuff in his truck and getting on with the plan. The truck was not Stumpy's. It was another duck hunter planning to cover the same water as he had planned on. This was the reason for the early start since this could happen anywhere. If this hunter's partner arrived before Stumpy, they would have to float another section of river or follow the other hunters. Following other hunters was sure to produce poor shooting. At 5:45 the other truck came and Evander resigned himself to floating the section of river above the Corpening Bridge, not a disaster, just not the best situation. He waited through dawn and until about 8:00. At that point he was worried about Stumpy being in a wreck, or worse. He went into town, found a pay phone, and called him at home. Stumpy answered the phone with sleep in his voice. "Are you OK?" Evander stammered.

"Sure, my brother came in from Charlotte yesterday and I decided not to go duck hunting. Did you get any ducks?"

Evander took a big breath. "I couldn't go. The reason we needed you to drive your truck was so we could get back to the other bridge to get my truck. You can't do it with just one vehicle."

Stumpy's voice was still full of sleep. "Oh, I never thought of that."

The next Sunday, I was at Evander's working on my boat when Stumpy drove up and asked Evander if he would help him sight in his deer rifle. "Sure," Evander said and picked up some targets and his spotting scope and walked down to the bench rest with Stumpy. When he returned and Stumpy had driven off, I asked Evander if they had discussed the aborted duck hunting trip. "No," was the answer.

"Aren't you going to chew him out?" I asked, incredulous.

"He'll learn better sometime," he shrugged. "When are you going to replace that prop?" When Evander changed the subject, it meant he was finished with the old one, and I respected his judgment.

Over a year later, we'd gone to Hatteras to visit with one of Evander's friends. It was just a few days before I had to go back to school from my time off for Christmas holiday and there was hardly anyone on the island. Frank Folb owned a tackle shop and spent his winters making sand spikes out of PVC pipe and pouring sinkers. I'd spent about half a day watching Frank pour hot molten lead into sinker moulds. Though it was about fifty degrees in the shop, Frank walked around the back of the tackle shop in shorts and deck shoes. My uncle sat on an old bait cooler and smoked cigars.

Frank and Evander talked about politics, availability of bait, island gossip, and all other kinds of things that were not interesting to me. As the afternoon dragged on, Evander sensed my growing discontent. "Let's take the truck and drive up the beach toward Rodanthe," he muttered. "This northwest wind may have blown some bait in for the stripers." I was ready for anything that would get me out of the cigar smoke and lead fumes.

We were just north of Avon when Evander chuckled. "Well, look at that! I believe we're in luck." I didn't know what he was talking about at first, but when I looked toward the ocean, I saw birds swarming everywhere. Evander did a U-turn, accelerated the old green Chevy, and headed for the closest ramp that would get us out on the beach. When we came over the top of the ramp, you could see the birds about a mile up the beach.

Evander sped up the beach with the old truck bouncing on its tired old shocks. The scene we approached could best be described as carnage. There were gannets dive bombing into the water from fifty feet up. When they hit, geysers of water spouted. The menhaden were there and the stripers were eating them. The porpoises were eating the menhaden or the stripers, I didn't know which, and the birds were cleaning up the stragglers and wounded. Evander moved fast, getting into his chest waders and then tying a spoon on the little rod he normally used for Spanish mackerel. "Get your waders on, Dick!" he shouted over the din of the screaming birds. "We're going to have to wade out to the bar."

The bar was about 75 feet out, and the water was calm between the beach and the breakers. On the other side of the breakers, pandemonium was happening. While I struggled into my waders, Evander tied a spoon on my smaller spinning rod. I noticed two more trucks pulling up. I knew how big ocean-run stripers were, and I was thinking we were under-gunned with the small rods, but I didn't question Evander. The old man beat me to the bar and made a cast. By the time I was starting my cast, I could see he had a fish on. I made my cast and was starting my retrieve, thinking how lucky he was to get a fish on the first cast when my line stopped coming in and started going out. I just held on and watched the line rolling off the spinning reel's spool. I looked up and noticed that there were now six people fishing and all were hooked up. There were more fishermen coming out to the bar. I realized the fight was not going to be quick and settled down for a protracted battle.

As I was leading my first big striper on metal back to the beach, I looked up and saw Evander's old, green truck coming down the beach. I guessed I was about a quarter mile further south than when I waded in and I was breathing hard. It was cold with a northeast wind blowing about twenty-five and I was sweating. I unhooked the fish and tried to put him in the cooler on the front of the truck. He wouldn't fit. Evander motioned for me to put him in the bed and I saw an even bigger one back there when I got around to the back of the Chevy.

Striper Run for Stumpy

Evander hollered, "C'mon! Let's go get another one!" and off we went. After the first two fish, it was catch and release, and we fished till it was too dark to see the birds. Evander drove back to Frank's, cleaned the fish, put most of it in the ice machine, and carried enough for about four people with us in a plastic bag. We pulled up to a place named Pop's with a picture of a sailor that looked like Popeye on the sign. We walked in. Evander set the bag of filets on the bar and winked at the waitress. She winked back, handed him a beer, and carried them into the kitchen. We waited on our dinner to be served.

As we consumed the best fish dinner I ever ate, Evander said. "This bite will happen again in the morning. The wind is going to blow this way for at least a day or two. When we get back to the motel we'll call Stumpy." I was amazed.

"Why are you going to call Stumpy?" I was incredulous.

"He's never caught a big striper before. This is almost a sure thing." The words were slightly muffled from the hushpuppies in Evander's mouth. I couldn't believe he was going to call this guy who'd cost him a whole day without so much as an apology. I'd learned that you don't argue with Evander Pritchert about his plans. I shifted my attention back to the golden fried striper fillets on my plate.

We ate breakfast at the Diamond Shoals restaurant the next morning. I loved eating there because there was a waitress named Donna with over forty rings on her fingers. I noticed them the first time she waited on us and Evander told me that her boyfriend was a pirate. At the time I was only eight, so I believed the story. Now I was older and knew better, but she was still a great mystery. As she served us our eggs, Evander told me Stumpy was leaving at three thirty this morning and would be down to meet us at the beach ramp at ten o'clock.

"I'll bet he don't show up!" I grumbled. Evander smiled.

After Evander finished his coffee, we got in the truck and went out on the beach to find the fish. It was easy; they were under the birds. We fished more leisurely today, following the fish down the beach until they went back out and then driving back up the beach to look for another school. We kept a couple more fish to bring home to the family for a fish fry. Ten o'clock came and went. At first, I didn't say anything, but after a while that strange urge that causes young men to say things just to be talking made me remind Evander that it was well past ten. Stumpy could not come to look for us because he didn't have four-wheel drive. At eleven thirty Evander said we'd better collect Stumpy.

Stumpy was sitting on the tailgate of his truck when we came over the ramp. He looked anxious, but he was polite and very glad to see us. He thanked Evander for inviting him and asked where to put his stuff. Evander apologized for being late and that there was no excuse for a man not keeping his word. Stumpy was quiet for a moment and then made a point of saying that it was no trouble at all.

Later, on the beach, as Stumpy and I released a couple of fish at the same time, he looked up at me and said, "Your uncle is quite a character; you're lucky to have him. I know what he did today and I had it coming."

I figured Stumpy would never stand Evander up again.

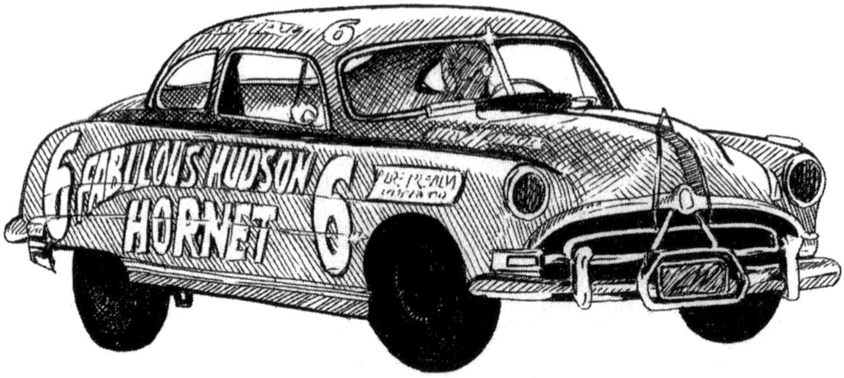
6
FABULOUS HUDSON
HORNET
6
6

Texas Trickery

My uncle, Evander Pritchert, made friends as easily as anyone I knew. Most of his friends were hunters, fishermen, and shooters, but some never wet a line or fired a gun. He managed to have something in common with everyone he met.

Two of those friends that didn't hunt or shoot were Slick Yarborough and Steve Lowe. They were involved with racing stock cars, and in fact, Slick was pretty good at it. I first met them at Wahoo's Restaurant one morning as Evander and I were going out to scout for a good dove field.

In those days, there were so many good places to dove hunt that the issue wasn't finding a place to hunt as it is now, but rather a matter of finding the best place to hunt. It seems that every good dove field I hunted over as a boy is now a housing development or a strip mall, but back then they were corn fields, rye fields, or tobacco fields that had been stripped of their cash-bearing crop and had flocks of mourning doves sailing over the forlorn stalks waiting to be plowed under.

I never quite understood what the doves saw

Texas Trickery

as an attraction in those tobacco stalks, but there was often great shooting to be had by standing along the edge of the "stripped" tobacco field in the tall grass or crouching under the last leaves to be pulled that we called "tips."

On this morning, Slick and Steve were sitting in a booth eating breakfast when Evander and I walked in and took seats on the stools at the counter. Everyone seemed to know Evander and I wasn't surprised when the two men started talking to Evander about all sorts of subjects from the fuel pump on Evander's old, green Chevy truck to how Steve cooked the best beef brisket east of the Pecos.

Slick told us he was buying Steve's breakfast to celebrate his birthday and asked us to join them in the booth to make conversation easier. The talk evolved from fuel pumps and beef brisket to Evander's last fishing trip, and during that part of the conversation, I figured out that, since they were both from Texas, they were bound to get high marks from Evander because he was always telling me that the friendliest Americans were Texans.

Then Steve began to reminisce about the first time he met Evander. It seems that Steve had gone to a meeting on Gaston Lake with a group of people from his racing team. One of the things on the schedule was a bank fishing tournament. Steve had taken a lot of ribbing from the other guys since he knew nothing of fishing and didn't even have a rod and reel. He'd bought one at the tackle shop the morning of the tournament and had asked one of the guys to show him how to use it.

When the fishing started, all the other guys wandered away from the marina to seek better fishing and left Steve struggling to work the rod

Texas Trickery

and reel. After several tangles and backlashes, he decided to just walk up to the hospitality tent and have a beer or two; there wasn't another soul there.

Eventually, he strolled down to the boat landing just at the time Evander was coming in from a morning of fishing. He was loading his boat and putting a stringer of stripers in the back of his truck. "Man, you caught a lot of fish today," Steve exclaimed. "You must really know how to fish. It's all I can do to work a rod and reel."

Evander smiled and said, "I'd have taken you with me if I'd known you wanted to learn how to fish." Evander saw the patch on Steve's shirt and asked, "Are you from Thomasville?" Steve explained that he was and that he was here with the racing team.

Evander told Steve that he was down there on a fishing trip for a couple of days and was from Thomasville, too. He was always offering what he'd caught to someone and asked, "Would you like these fish to carry home?"

At first, Steve declined, but then he got an idea. "Yeah, I'd like to have 'em." He smiled and took the fish.

The next day, Evander was again loading his boat at the marina when Steve strolled up carrying a really nice rod and reel. He handed it to Evander and smiled, "Here's your prize."

Evander was bumfuzzled. "What prize?" he asked.

"I won the fishing contest for the biggest fish and the most fish. I got a hundred dollars for the most fish and that rod for the biggest fish. The rod is your part of the winnings," Steve chuckled, smiling from ear to ear.

Texas Trickery

As we left the restaurant, Steve went on out to the car while Slick paid. Once he was gone, Slick said, "Why don't you boys come to my place tonight for Steve's surprise birthday party? We're having beef brisket with all the fixin's. Dick can find out what Texas barbeque is all about."

Evander was puzzled. "Who's cooking the brisket? Steve would complain about any brisket but his."

"Oh, Steve's cooking the brisket," Slick grinned. "I told him I needed three briskets for a party at the wrecking yard. That's why he's in such a hurry; he wants to get back to check on 'em," Slick laughed.

As the two Texans pulled out of the parking lot, Evander muttered, "And that's why they call him Slick!"

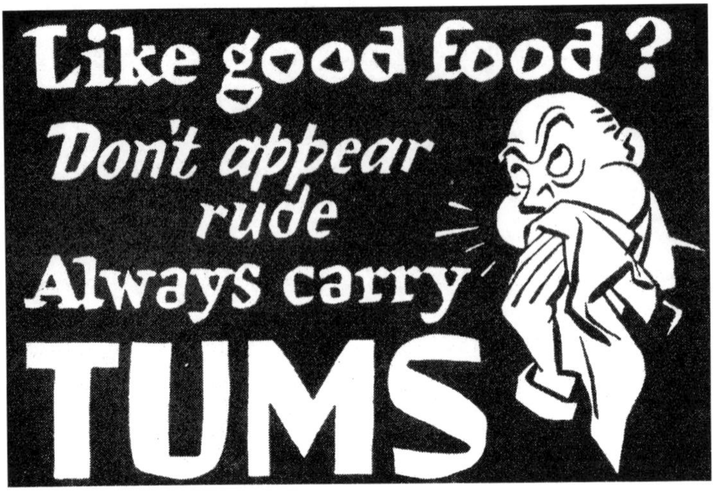
Like good food?
Don't appear rude
Always carry
TUMS

The Lie as Art

My uncle Evander was a patient man. He had to be to deal with me tangling his lines, dropping his stuff, getting hung on the bottom when we were fishing, and unlimited other dumb things that inexperienced fishermen and hunters do. He could tell some of the wildest tales that have ever been told, but I trusted him as much as anyone I knew who was over 20.

I trusted him because I knew that, if I really needed information, he'd supply it. He never told me a serious lie, but he told me thousands of funny ones. Early on, we developed a system. If I wasn't sure if he was pulling my leg or not, and I really wanted to know, I would just say, "Are you telling the truth?" He promised me I'd always get the truth then and I don't think that he ever deceived me under those circumstances. When you are somewhere between 8 and 18, the real truth is a valuable thing, and I always got it from him if I prefaced the question with that phrase.

Although he had little use for a liar for profit or a bragging liar, he was polite, pretending

The Lie as Art

he believed what he heard. I never heard him call someone a liar, or so I thought. We were at a gunshop in the part of the state called "down east." Evander had given me a North Carolina Rifle Team hat and I was wearing it. As we walked into the gunshop, a loud man standing at the gun counter noticed my hat. "Son, so you shoot on the state rifle team?" he asked.

"No, sir," I answered.

"Well, my friend does and he won the Long Range State Championship this year and he used my rifle."

Evander smiled. "How is Tom doing?" Evander asked. I was thinking of the hot day in July that I'd been on the range with Evander and Tom Whealton. They'd shot on the same target on different relays, and Evander had won the Service Rifle Championship while Tom had won the Match Rifle Championship. They'd taken some friendly ribbing about it since they had scored each other's targets.

The man's face darkened. "Tom? Tom who? My friend's name is Jack Stark. He shot my rifle, a 7mm Remington Magnum."

Evander looked apologetic, "I'm sorry. I thought you were talking about the Long Range State Championships held at Camp Butner this July."

The loud man said, "That's the match. He shot my rifle, I loaded the ammunition for him, and he shot a perfect score. I built the rifle myself."

Evander looked at me and smiled. "Well, that's just incredible," he said politely and began a conversation with the man he had come to see.

When we got back to the truck, I asked

The Lie as Art

Evander why he didn't call out the loud man for lying, since we both knew his friend and his rifle didn't win at the state championship.

"Why, Dick, I did call him a liar." And he gave me a wink. "Look up the word 'incredible' in the dictionary."

Evander saw lying as an art to be practiced for the joy of it. He considered lying for profit evil, and if he knew you did it, you didn't stay close to him long. He demanded honesty from his friends on serious matters as a condition of friendship. He had the utmost respect for someone who could fool him as a matter of a joke though, and he'd buy your lunch if you got a good one on him.

He was proud of his wife, my aunt Dianne, for many things; she could outshoot and out-fish most of the men, she was smart, and she was pretty. But I never saw him as proud of her as he was when she pulled a prank on him. There was one prank she pulled on him that he told about a hundred times. He could have not been more proud of her if she had figured out how to turn water into gasoline.

Old Bob was Evander's lab, and sometimes, Bob had bad breath. He always sat in the back seat of Evander's old GMC Jimmy and hung his head over the seat back when they were traveling. Evander didn't mind it; he hardly had a sense of smell anyway, but Aunt Dianne couldn't stand the smell of canine bad breath. She found a mail order place that sold dog breath mints, and she bought some and put them in the glove compartment of the Jimmy.

They'd gone to Hatteras for some fishing, and I'd been allowed to go along. It had been a great trip, we had caught fish, I'd found some great

The Lie as Art

shells to bring to Mom, and we were on our way home. On our last day, we fished till nine in the morning, straightened up the gear and stowed it, and packed up to go home. We stopped at Pop's Seafood Restaurant, on Highway 12, to eat an early lunch before we left. Pop's had the best fried scallops I've had anywhere in all my travels, and my uncle loved them, too. Aunt Dianne warned him that they would cause him to get indigestion while driving, but he just gave me a wink and ordered them anyway.

By the time we had gotten up Highway 64 to Roper, the indigestion hit my uncle with full force. He shifted uncomfortably in his seat, he burped, he took long breaths, and finally he gave up. He knew that Aunt Dianne normally carried Tums in her purse, and as much as he hated admitting that she had been right about eating the fried scallops and then driving, he desperately needed the Tums. Finally he asked. "Do you have any Tums? You were right dear, the indigestion has hit me."

She turned and looked at me in the back seat with Bob and smiled; she winked. "I knew it would, I have some right here," she replied. She looked at me again and winked. I had no idea what she was doing. She handed Evander the tablet and watched. There was a certain triumphant look on her face. Evander chewed the tablet and began to make a face, he gagged and then rolled the window down and began to spit out the window and hack like he had a fur ball.

"What was that?" he demanded.

"It was one of Bob's dog breath mints; how did it taste?" By now she was laughing so hard that tears were rolling down her face. I was laughing too, and if old Bob had understood, he would have been laughing.

Evander was now laughing harder than either of us. "That was a good one," he chuckled, catching his breath, "and that is why I love you so."

The Value of Time

My Uncle Evander was the busiest man I've ever known, but since he always had time to talk, most folks thought he did nothing. He had a job of sorts, he would get a phone call, talk to the person on the other line about switches, cylinders, and valves, and the next thing I knew he would be gone somewhere for a week. When he came back he would be talking about fishing for salmon in Lake Michigan or going crabbing with someone in the Puget Sound.

His daily routine consisted of fixing things around his place, meeting someone for lunch, and then working in his shop with a myriad of strange looking machines mixed in with boat accessories, shotshell loaders, fishing gear, and whatever hunting or fishing project he was working on. He made his own boat blind that worked like a store-bought blind. He refitted his boat to have components that could be removed and replaced and allowed him to use the same boat for fresh and salt water and as a recreational boat and a hunting boat with the aforementioned duck hunting blind.

The Value of Time

He would talk to a friend he ran into at a restaurant as if he had nothing else to do and then rush off to the next project like his tail was afire. He tried to teach every kid he ran into to fish and shoot, took a lot of them on trips, and was constantly doing something for his gun club, or church, or some other group.

I knew he enjoyed being idle. When we went on a fishing trip, he would sit for hours on the beach watching a surf rod, smoking a cigar, and talking about anything I wanted to talk about. We'd kill three or four days doing practically nothing, and when he got home, he got busy again just as he'd been the week before we left. As a young man, I just didn't understand what drove him so to do all the different things that kept him so busy.

"Why do you have so many things to do?" I asked one day when I was at his shop while he was working on a disc harrow that belonged to a neighbor.

"There's a lot of things that need to get done," he replied absently, knocking the slag off a still smoking weld.

"But that's not your disc; it's Bo's disc. Why don't you let Bo fix it? Bo can weld can't he?"

He stopped, took off the welding helmet, found his cigar on the work bench, and relit it. "Bo can't weld as well as I can. If he fixes it, it'll just break again. He plows your aunt's garden and it's the least I could do. What kind of a neighbor would I be if I didn't help out my friends?"

I quit bugging him and went back outside to pet the dogs and remembered an earlier conversation. We'd been driving and he always got philosophical when we went on long trips. "Some folks say a man

The Value of Time

comes into the world with nothing and leaves it with nothing. They don't know what they're talking about," he said. I knew that for the next 50 or so miles, I was going to get an education.

"When we come into the world, we have one thing, time. Time is all we have to trade for our food and shelter. When you take a job or plant a crop, you trade your time for money and you use that money to buy comfort. Some folks store up money thinking that money will keep them from ever having to do without comfort. Sometimes that works. Some folks just don't like to work and give up the comfort so they don't have to." He tossed a short section of cigar out the window and rolled it up.

He said, "I see my time as a gift, I don't know how much I've got here and I want to spend it like you do when you get a dollar to spend at the fair." I thought of how carefully I'd budgeted myself at the fair to get maximum use out of the money Daddy had given me. "I trade some of my time for money, I spend some on you, I spend some on friends, and I use some of it to do things for other people. Some folks say you leave this world with nothing, but that's not true. You leave this world with the knowledge that you meant something to the people you left. I know where I'm going when I leave here and I just want the people around me to miss me when I leave."

"I don't want to waste my time here on something that means nothing to anybody," Evander went on. "So I do things I don't have to do. I could waste my time doing stuff that wouldn't amount to a hill of beans, but what kind of man would I be if I spent all my spare time watching television. I'd be like Charlie Starke."

The Value of Time

Charlie Starke was a man who never quite grew up. He was interested only in what was of benefit to him and would only do something for someone else if it was profitable to him. Evander explained that Charlie wasn't very happy because it's hard to be happy when you only care about yourself. Evander's theory was that happiness comes from doing things for someone else, not yourself. Charlie was always complaining about how people never did anything for him, though quite often, they had. He just couldn't see someone's kindness for what it was. I remembered how he'd told me about Charlie and the pigs and apples when I was a few years younger.

It seems that Charlie had a grove of apple trees on his farm. The grove of trees was along the road and Evander happened to be driving by one day and saw Charlie standing under a tree holding a pig up. He pulled into the little tractor road that ran just off the end of the apple orchard and walked out to where Charlie was standing, holding a pig up while it ate an apple.

"What in the devil are you doing, Charlie?" Evander was amazed.

"Apples ain't bringing enough this year to bother picking them so I'm letting the pigs have them," Charlie grunted.

"Why don't you call the church and let the church kids pick the apples? They could sell them and use the money for a trip or something. They'd have a ball picking, and you'd have done something nice." Evander was always thinking up schemes like that.

"Naw," he growled. "One of 'em would probably fall out of a tree and they'd sue me. I'm just going to let the pigs eat 'em."

"Well," Evander said, "if you're going to let the pigs eat the apples, why don't you just shake the tree and let the pigs eat the apples off the ground? It'd save a lot of time."

Charlie looked at Evander as if he were an idiot. "What's time to a pig?" he said.

Evander shook his head and started back for the truck. "Yeah, I guess you're right. I don't know what I was thinking."

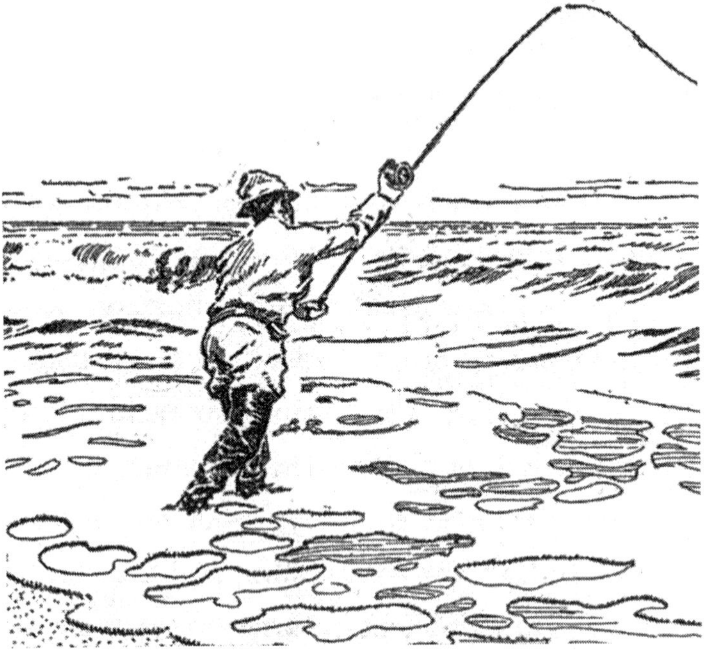

Vinny and Roxanne and the Two Way Radios

My Uncle Evander Prichart was not a high tech guy. He didn't trust computers or electronic gadgets. He didn't even trust automatic shotguns or spinning reels. He would use one if he had to, but he didn't care for them. His old, green Chevy truck had points and a carburetor and he was proud of the fact. When I showed him my new Silverado he liked the nice features, but he reminded me that if his truck broke he could fix it and that it would take an engineer to get mine going again.

When he showed up just before a week-long beach trip to Hatteras with a pair of brand new Motorola two-way radios, I was shocked. "These things are great," he beamed. "My buddy, Bob, uses them to shuttle school buses cross country and he says that they'll carry twice as far as a CB. We can talk to each other driving down and while we're on the beach." I just shook my head.

The radios did work great. We always drove separate trucks when we surf fished so we could fish independently. Sometimes Evander wanted to fish more than I did. I'd learned that if we were in one truck, I was likely to spend the night sleeping on a truck seat while my bed at the beach house was empty.

As I followed him down to the outer banks, we found that we could talk when we were a couple of miles apart, and there was no interference since these VHF radios were new to the market. We chatted all the way down Highway 64 and NC 12 until we were in Avon.

We picked up bait at Frank and Fran's, groceries at the Connors IGA, and went to the house. Evander had traded a Model 12 Skeet Winchester for a week in a really nice beach house on the beachfront.

We unloaded the groceries and were getting ready to go out on the beach when his radio squawked. "Roxanne, can you just bring me a sandwich and a beer? I'm catching blues and I want to keep fishing."

The radio crackled again. "Sure Vinnie, I'll be right there." The voices had an unmistakable New Jersey accent. Evander was never bashful; he picked up his radio and asked Vinnie where he was fishing. The radio went silent; Vinnie never answered.

We spent the next couple of hours cutting bait, spooling reels, organizing our trucks and getting ready for a hard week of fishing. Evander seemed troubled by the non-response on the radio, but he didn't talk about it.

Though we heard Vinnie and Roxanne talk through the next week, they would never respond to Evander when he'd ask them if they were catching anything or if he volunteered information about where we were fishing and what we were catching.

Vinny and Roxanne and the Two Way Radios

Evander didn't give up easily. When we got into a school of little blues that were hitting every Hopkins lure we tossed out, he picked up the radio and advised Vinnie of where we were and what was happening. There was no return response.

As we fished, I noticed him looking at the trucks that went by, as if he was waiting for Vinnie and Roxanne to drive up so he could talk to them in person. It never happened.

This was a serious breach of civility in Evander's world. He was the kind of guy who talked to everyone like they were family. That kind of behavior is considered strange in New York City, but Evander wasn't interested in how things were done in New York; he was a son of the gentle South.

He never ordered food without some kind of conversation with the waitress or waiter. There would always be the normal greeting from the server, and he would come back with a joke or something that disrupted the polite but uncaring conversation that normally ensues when people are forced to converse when they really don't care to. By the time he ordered, he would know something about the servers, and they would know something about him.

Sometimes, the conversation would cause them to miss part of the order and when that happened, he would gently remind them of the discrepancy, calling them by their name. He often would walk out of a restaurant overjoyed that the people who'd served him had not been shy about talking. If he returned to the same restaurant, he would make a point to speak to his new friend, whether they were waiting on him or not.

I suppose some people he talked to thought

of him as a strange old man. I know many actually enjoyed finding someone who wasn't afraid to talk and the practice made him countless friends. Sometimes we'd go duck hunting at someone's beaver pond behind the family farm and I'd ask, "How do you know these folks?"

He'd shrug his shoulders and mumble something about buying windshield wipers at NAPA and then establish some distant relationship his new friends had with some of his older friends, maybe the ones he met at the feed store buying chickens.

I think we've really lost something in our modern society. We watch shows on TV that center around life in New York and Los Angeles and a lot of us try to pretend we live there. We forget our roots and worry about strangers, considering them as threats and avoiding looking them in the eye. I think we've lost a lot by creating this distance between us and strangers.

On the last night before we left, Vinnie and Roxanne were sitting comfortably in their rented beach house. A Nor'easter had blown in and the wind was gusting to thirty knots. It was raining big drops sideways. Vinnie had just finished a bowl of soup when the radio crackled.

"Dick, you better get out here! I just caught my second drum and both were over forty-eight inches!"

My voice came on the radio. "Where are you?"

Evander came back, "Just below ramp thirty-four in the hole we fished this afternoon."

Vinnie dropped his soup bowl in the sink and put on his yellow slicker as he went down the steps to his truck.

Minutes later, Vinnie was driving up and down the beach below ramp thirty-four as waves crashed in the pitch dark. His wipers were slashing furiously at the spray, sand, and rain that lashed across his windshield. "Evander, Dick, how far below thirty-four are you?"

"Do you want some more coffee to go with that pound cake?" my uncle asked as he stood in thick wool socks in the spacious kitchen of our borrowed beach house. I was sitting in a leather recliner. My stocking feet were aimed toward the gas log fireplace as I nodded in the affirmative.

The radio crackled again. "Hey, Dick, how far below thirty-four are you guys?" Vinnie's voice was unmistakable. I pictured Vinnie driving around on the hostile beach in rain and howling winds.

Evander topped up my coffee cup and clicked the Motorola off. He winked and said, "Well, would you look at that? Vinnie's gotten friendly enough to talk to strangers."

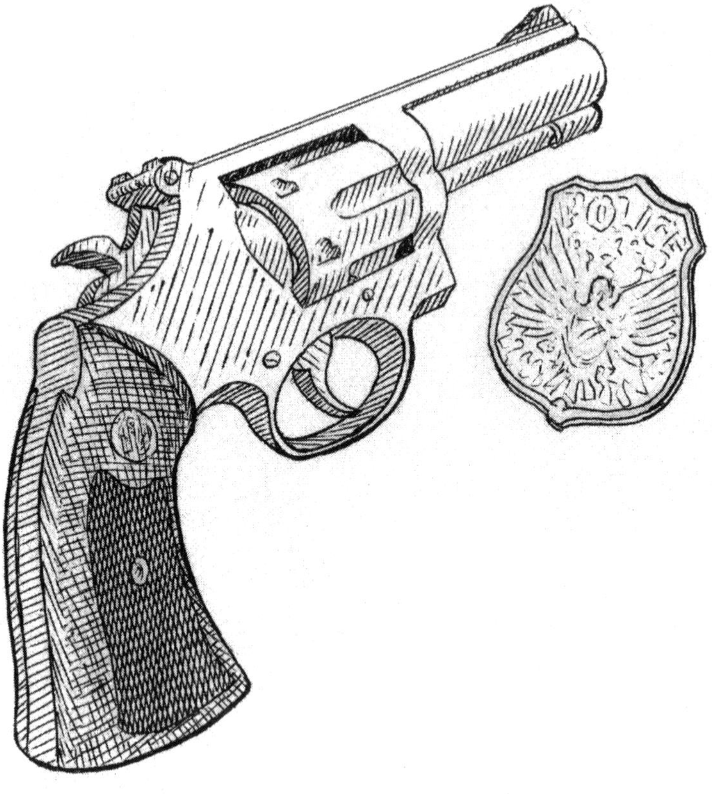

White Ford Lies

The truck was a white Ford 150 with four-wheel drive, manual transmission, a V8 engine, and more dog hair in the interior than any truck I've ever seen. It was a Ford interruption in the line of green Chevy trucks that Uncle Evander owned. As all of Evander's trucks, it smelled of wet Labrador retriever and stale cigar smoke. The seating arrangement was the normal deal, with me riding shotgun, Bob, Evander's fox red lab, in the center sitting on the armrest with his front feet on the edge of the seat, and Evander behind the wheel.

Evander was talking about fishing and eating a tenderloin biscuit. He stopped talking and developed a look of intense concentration on his face. He worked a small piece of fat to the front of his mouth and picked it out. He passed it to Bob's waiting mouth and resumed the conversation. "What was I talking about?" He needed help to get back into the lesson he was giving me on the ride to the river.

"You were talking about folks telling lies," I answered.

"I just don't see why guys have to tell lies to impress other folks. If you only caught four fish, say you just caught four fish. Smart people will know you're being honest and appreciate it. Dumb folks'll probably think you're not that good a fisherman and won't ask you to take 'em fishing. Life's too short to fish with dumb people, anyway." He fished a big cigar out of his vest pocket, bit the end off, and struck up his fancy lighter.

Evander's lighter was a subject of discussion wherever he got it out. It looked like a scuba tank and roared like a jet engine. He could light a cigar underwater in a hurricane with that thing. The flame was blue-hot, and I once saw him solder a wire on a boat with it. He puffed and smoke chugged out of him and the cigar; always considerate, he rolled his window down about an inch and the smoke evaporated out the window.

"You tell lies all the time," I said. "Everybody knows you're the biggest liar in the county." When I said this, I knew the difference; Evander's lies were for fun and entertainment. He was scrupulously honest about whether the fish were biting, how many ducks he got, or how many shells he used getting his limit of doves.

"You know what I'm talking about," he snorted. "Remember that fella that told us he'd caught his limit of stripers the other week? I knew better and he should've known better than to tell the lie; he insulted my intelligence with such a tale. What if he'd told someone who didn't know better? The next fella would have told someone else and it would've spread the lie so by Saturday you couldn't get on the river for the crowd. Stuff like that blows up like gas on a brush-pile."

I was enjoying the conversation and wanted to keep it going. Bob suddenly whipped his head around and whined. We were passing a pond where we'd shot some ducks last year. There were a few wood ducks sitting on the pond. I was always amazed how that dog knew where we were at any given moment and would start looking for a pond or river a quarter mile before we got there. I threw out more bait, "Aw, lies like that don't really hurt anything." I knew this would keep Evander going on the subject for at least another half hour. We'd had this conversation before and it was one of his favorites.

"Don't hurt anything!" he exclaimed... and we both saw the Warren County Sherriff's car nestled back in the trees. Evander glared at the speedometer; he sighed. "Now I've gone and talked myself into a ticket." The brown and white Ford was pulling out on to the highway with lights flashing. The look of irritation changed. He chuckled, "You just don't say anything no matter what I say." He looked at me with his strange combination of stern mischief. "This is an opportunity for you to learn something."

Evander pulled off the road, rolled the window down, and waited for the deputy. The deputy looked only a few years older than me; he looked like he could've been my school bus driver. "Mornin, Officer," Evander seemed unnaturally relaxed.

The deputy seemed more nervous than Evander. "Can I see your license?" His tone was businesslike.

Evander looked straight ahead. "I don't have one," he answered. I knew better but kept my mouth shut as instructed.

"May I see your registration?" The deputy seemed more nervous.

White Ford Lies

"I don't know where it is. You see, I just stole this truck this morning and haven't had a chance to look for it." Evander still hadn't looked the deputy in the face. If he had, he'd have noticed that the deputy was really getting agitated. I was afraid we were going to get shot.

"Would you step out of the truck, Sir?" The deputy was definitely rattled now,

"I'd rather not," Evander said. "I'm so drunk I'm not sure I could stand up." At this, I started to speak up, and Evander gave me a stern look. I sat back.

The deputy walked back to the patrol car and got on the radio. "What are you doing?" I asked. "We're supposed to go fishing and you're going to get us arrested."

Within minutes, we were surrounded by squad cars. A beefy man with a red face approached the truck on the driver's side. I saw a surprised look on his face and something about him was familiar, I wondered if I'd seen him on TV. He was the sheriff for sure.

"Could I see your driver's license?" he asked politely.

"Certainly," Evander said cordially and handed him the license.

"Could I see your registration?" the sheriff looked puzzled.

"Of course," Evander replied and pulled it off the visor.

The sheriff examined the registration and slowly shook his head. "I'll assume that you haven't been drinking," the sheriff said casually.

"Of course not," Evander said, still dead serious.

White Ford Lies

The sheriff was stern. "Evander Pritchert, my deputy said you had no license, that the truck was stolen, and that you're drunk. None of this is true. What do you have to say and what is this all about?" I recognized the sheriff's face now. He owned the pond we'd just passed, and he'd hunted the wood ducks with us last year. I just knew him as John, from Warren County, and hadn't known he was the sheriff. I breathed a sigh of relief.

Evander puffed the cigar back to life. "He said all that? If he said that, John, he must be a liar and he probably told you I was speeding, too!"

Evander looked me and said, "See what I was talking about?"

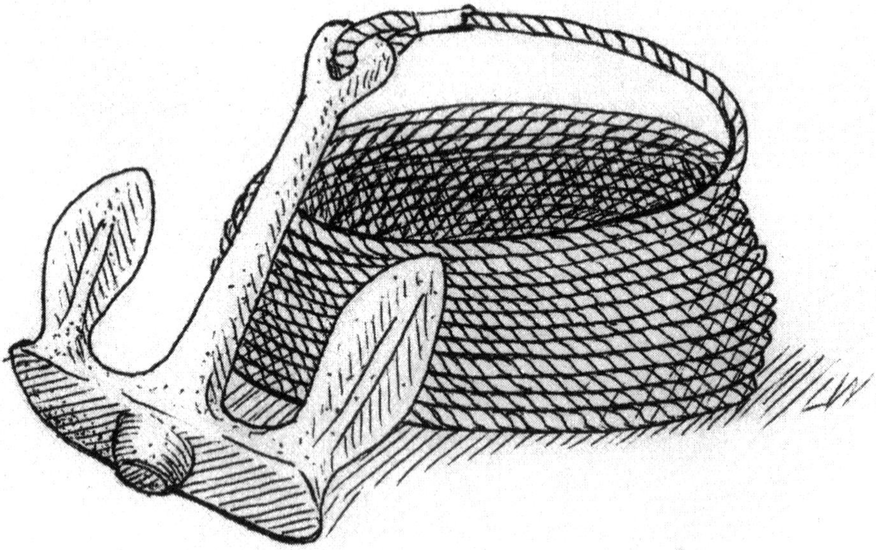

William Angel

Uncle Evander had an appropriate phrase for every situation that could ever happen. Most were the normal, commonly used statements that you hear every day, but some were unusual. One I remember most was when someone did something that was profitable but wrong and escaped consequences, Evander would say "Every tub sits on its own bottom." I never quite understood that one, but he said it like everyone had heard it and knew it. If you were around Evander for more than an hour, you would hear one of his pearls.

William Angel was an imperfectly formed child. He was about 30 years old when my uncle met him and, while he was strong and agile physically, he just never grew up past about twelve years in mind. He had an eternal smile that exposed teeth that could have been a lot better maintained and he was almost always happy. William had a slight speech impediment that made him seem even more childlike and his boundless energy reinforced that conclusion.

William worked at the ice plant, at Turner's

Fish House, on the wharf in New Orleans, where Uncle Evander lived at the time. My uncle never met a stranger and William's innocent smile won him over right away. William's parents had moved to Grand Isle, and since Evander had a fishing and hunting camp there, it was only logical that Evander would wind up giving William a ride sometimes when he was going down there to hunt or fish. Obviously, William was exposed to a lot of Evander's axioms and, the fact that he was, is the basis of this strange tale.

Big Dan Turner was the owner and operator of the fish house where most of the French Quarter's restaurants bought the seafood that they served every day. It was not a monopoly, but Turner's operation was more convenient than any other supplier, and the business relationship was good. Evander bought all the seafood for his little restaurant there and as a result, knew about everything that went on around the fish house.

Dan Turner had a daughter off in college when Evander first met him, and when she graduated, she went to work at the fish house running the retail side of the operation. Jane, or Janie, as she was called at the fish house, was a tall, pretty girl, not a beauty queen, but wholesome and with big blue eyes. She always got a second look from someone meeting her for the first time.

William saw Jane three or four times a day since it was his job to keep ice in the display cases, and Jane always spoke to him and smiled when he came in the room. While William was childlike in many ways, he was a man, and Jane was a pretty girl who treated him well, so the attraction was only natural. Jane had no idea at first that he was attracted to her, but eventually she noticed it and didn't exactly know how to handle his attention.

About the time all this was happening, young Robert Thibodaux came back to the quarter. Robert worked as a fishing guide in Florida during the winter and, once his fishing clients were driven north by the intense heat, he worked as first mate on his brothers shrimp boat out of Delacroix. The Thibodaux brothers sold shrimp to Big Dan so Robert and Jane were bound to meet. On this occasion, the attraction was mutual.

Robert began to find excuses to spend time in the quarter, and the two were often seen together in restaurants and coffee houses and walking on the quay holding hands. This was devastating for William even though he'd always liked Robert. William had worked at the fish house for several years, and Robert had always been nice to him even giving him gifts on occasion. Now Robert was between him and the object of his affection, and his jealousy was driving him crazy.

On his trips home in Evander's truck, he vented. "Why does she like him better than me?" William wailed in despair, "I found her before he did." Evander tried to explain that sometimes people were attracted to one person more than someone else and that was just the way it was. This was little consolation for William, who pouted and fretted so much that Evander worried that he might lose his job. In the mean time, Jane tried to console William as much as possible without increasing his ardor.

The romance bloomed through the summer and Robert and Jane were seen even more often as the fall approached and the time for Robert to return to Florida drew near. William seemed to be taking it better and when Evander remarked on this on one of the trips to Grand Isle, William smiled broadly and replied, "I have a plan." He couldn't be persuaded to reveal the plan, but he had such a sweet nature that Evander wasn't too concerned.

Robert was very well liked in the Quarter, and in those days, the Quarter was a small, close knit community. It was traditional for Robert's friends to meet at Kaldi's Coffee House on Robert's last day in New Orleans for a send off party. Robert had coffee and a sweet roll there every morning that he wasn't on the shrimp boat, and today, he was leaving at noon. William walked in with a huge grin and an even bigger box and Evander was glad to see him showing so much affection for Robert.

He insisted that Robert open the present immediately, and when it was opened, all those who could see in the box looked totally baffled. As Robert told William that the gift was too nice but that it would come in handy, Evander positioned himself to see what was inside. It was a huge coil of anchor rope. William proudly blurted that it was a new anchor line for Robert's flats boat.

Robert explained to William that he only need about 50 feet of anchor line on the flats boat since he never anchored in deep water and that, perhaps, William would like to take some of it back and get some of his money back. William refused saying that you just never know when you're going to need to anchor in deep water and that it might come in handy. To Evander's experienced ear, the explanation sounded a little rehearsed.

Evander forgot about the incident for a couple of weeks until another trip to Grand Isle came up and William was riding in the truck with him. "William, why did you give Robert the anchor line?" Evander figured that a quick direct shot would be likely to get a more honest response.

"Robert was going to come back next spring" William blurted.

"What does the anchor line have to do with that?" Evander shot back.

William grinned, "I told you I had a plan."

Now Evander was cautious, "What kind of a plan?"

"Robert's not coming back next spring." Williams smile was now conspiratorial. "You gave me the idea."

"And what idea was that? Evander was now totally confused.

William was triumphant. "You told me that if you give a man enough rope, he'll hang himself!"

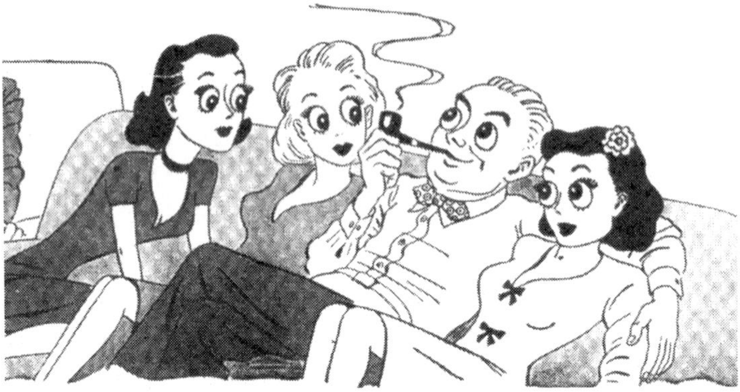

Dave and Toots and the Ivory Box

Evander Prichart was not one to shy away from adventure. He was also not one to meet a stranger. In the seventies, he was shooting NRA High Power Rifle matches, and during that time, he made a lot of friends. In those days at Camp Perry where the National Championships were held, rifle shooters were forced to make a lot of friends. The ranges ran seven relays of shooters, and when you weren't on the line shooting or scoring, you were in the pits pulling and marking targets. All this suited my uncle just fine because it gave him an excuse to make more friends.

He told stories and jokes until people who were normally quiet started to join the party. Hi-power rifle shooters have always been known as a social lot, but Evander kicked it up to serious fun. Most of the shooters stayed in little fourteen foot square huts called hooches. Evander always brought cooking gear and would set up a table outside his hooch and prepare huge dinners for friends old and recent. Often, the people that he shot with today had dinner with him tonight.

The dinners consisted of the kind of food he cooked in the field or on the boat, but it was nothing to be scoffed at. He would grill chickens, have fish fries, stir fry Japanese food, or perhaps make a big pot of chicken Creole. He was not intimidated by the fact that there was no running water or refrigeration at the hut, since he was used to cooking on boats or shooting trips.

These impromptu dinners brought all sorts of personalities together. Lawyers would eat with machinists and military shooters. Preachers would sit down to a meal with men who, at home, ran strip clubs. Evander liked all types of people and fit in with them all. He never worried about how they would get along, and so they just did.

One of the more memorable of those shooting friends was Dave Williquette. Dave was short, had a pot belly, a bald head, and a voice like gravel sliding around in a washtub. Dave also was a ladies man. Under normal conditions, Dave's expression was a sort of cheerful scowl. When a pretty girl or woman was around, he developed the expression of a delightful child. His voice softened, he became the most polite person you ever saw, and he made idle conversation as though he had no ulterior motives at all. When the attractive female left his presence, he made it known where she rated on a scale of one to ten and what kind of plans he had for her. This seemed humorous to those who didn't know him well because he was an unlikely suitor, but he had an amazing track record of success. Evander told me once that women have an uncanny knack for seeing a man as he sees himself, and this must have worked in Dave's favor.

Dave was from Oshkosh, Wisconsin, and he

Dave and Toots and the Ivory Box

had the Midwestern accent in spades. When he had been drinking, the gravelly voice got louder, and he would sometimes recount some of his conquests. Some of the stories got pretty wild, but Evander found that if you confronted him about some detail that didn't quite sound right, he'd confess and tell you the truth whether it made him look good or not. Evander found this to be a rather profound type of honesty since most men when confronted would just as soon die for the honor of their lie. He liked Dave very much.

While Camp Perry was 95% men during the National Matches, it was still in many ways a "target rich environment," as Dave said. There were women working in the various support offices that are required to make something like the biggest match in the world work, and a lot of those women were there to meet a man. At first glance Dave might not be seen as a "catch", but once you saw him in action, you realized that he saw himself as one. He had a very good job, a nice car, and he traveled on business and had lots of stories. He owned a nice house in Oshkosh and had a swimming pool. The pool was a source of great pride for him, and he made a lot of references to it, especially in the Ohio August heat. Evander imagined that if the pool could talk it could tell some interesting stories. While Dave really did have the house with the pool and the Corvette, the girls at Camp Perry never saw them. It made no difference. The level of confidence was there and apparently it was powerful.

Dave would have a girlfriend by the second or third day of the matches, and she would always be a pretty and charming woman. People who didn't know Dave would marvel at this. Those that did would wink knowingly. The relationship would appear to those not knowing Dave as one with a lot of potential to become permanent. But after the matches it would wither. The amazing part was that when he saw last year's girlfriend this year, she would act like an old and cherished friend and sometimes introduce him to this year's girl friend. It was a mystery.

One year, Dave came to Camp Perry with a wedding band on his finger. This created a lot of quiet conversation in fourteen foot square hooches. He said he'd met her last fall and that she was the woman for him. He had a photo. She was very attractive, but about his age. Dave normally had girlfriends that were younger than him. We watched him closely to see if the old Dave would arise in the environment where he had functioned so well in the past, but he was a perfect husband.

Old girlfriends were noticeably shaken but while they hugged and congratulated him, it was easy to see their disappointment. Everything about him was the same except the "hunting dog" persona. Strangely, that aspect was such a large part of his personality that he seemed much smaller without it. He shot very well, "probably because he was getting more sleep," someone joked.

That fall, Evander drove up to spend a few days with Dave to usher in the duck and goose season. On arrival, Evander met Toots, Dave's new bride. She was a stunningly attractive woman who was friendly enough and seemed to adore Dave.

The amazing thing was that she was more of an outdoorsman than either of them. She had a cabinet full of the nicest guns you have ever seen. She had a row of English doubles, mostly sidelocks, from light game guns to fowlers and a pair of nice Greener pigeon guns. She had graded Foxes in all three gauges, Model 70s in a variety of calibers, even a model 70 African in .458. She was an accomplished fisherman. Evander was amazed.

Not only did Toots have nice guns and tackle, she was as beautiful as any woman Evander had ever seen. True, she was not young, but youth is not always required for beauty. She was slim where a woman should be and well-blessed in the other parts of her anatomy. Further, she was natured like one of the guys. It seemed that she was not even conscious that she was a beautiful woman. Evander rarely coveted someone's wife, but it was difficult to not feel that Toots was much more woman than Dave deserved. Evander thought that he had met the perfect woman.

Later, when Toots had gone to the store, Dave filled Evander in. Her father had been a buyer for Abercrombie and Fitch in its glory days. He had access to all sorts of stuff and had taken Toots on trips all over the world. "Don't shoot against her for money," Dave warned, "She'll clean your plow. Did you look closely at the flies in that flybox?"

Evander was not big on fly fishing, but Dave was. "I saw them, they were perfect," Evander said, worried that Dave was going to get off on fly fishing. He could talk for hours about the subject. Evander owned fly rods, but he was not an aficionado.

"She tied them. I've begged her to tie me some of them, but she says that when she was a girl, her dad made her tie them for his friends and she hates doing it. She refuses to do it anymore," Dave said sadly.

Dave knew a lot of the local farmers in the

Dave and Toots and the Ivory Box

area, and he, Evander, and Toots shot geese and ducks with a lot of success. Toots called geese and ducks like a down-east guide. She shot like one, too. They hunted grouse in the hills over Abby, Dave's sweet old chocolate lab, and even deer hunted a couple of afternoons, something Evander rarely did. Dave was really impressed with Evander's rifle. It was a Custom Mauser in seven millimeter. It was a little modern looking for Evander, who leaned toward plain Model 70 Winchesters, but it was slender and light, and the action was smooth as melted butter. The stock was beautiful French walnut with fine checkering, and the bluing on the slender barrel was polished and perfectly done.

Dave was a pretty good cook, and the three of them took turns cooking. They had a pretty good time in the evenings with the three of them hunting ducks or geese in the mornings, walking up a few grouse after lunch, and sometimes hunting deer in the afternoons. When the guns were put away, Dave would ask Toots to make them a "cocktail". Dave could handle his liquor, but Evander was amazed to see that Toots could even out-drink him.

Dave tried to buy the Mauser. Evander hadn't had it long and didn't really want to sell it. A few days later Dave tried to trade Evander a little Winchester 101 20 gauge for it. Evander had tried to buy the 101 from him on the last trip, and Dave had refused to sell it. Evander had just bought one like it, so that didn't work.

Every day after that, Dave tried to get Evander to sell him the gun, but Evander refused. Everything else about the trip went well. The ducks flew into the little potholes Dave knew about, and Abby did a great job on the grouse and woodcock in

Dave and Toots and the Ivory Box

the thickets. The three of them got together with a bunch of guys from Dave's plant and had a pheasant drive and took turns cooking great dinners at Dave's house with the swimming pool.

On the last night, things got strange. Toots insisted that Dave go into town and get some spinach for what she was fixing for dinner. Evander was a great judge of character and sensed something was going on. Sure enough, as soon as Dave was down the drive way, Toots walked into the den where Evander was, sat down on the couch with him and told him she wanted the Mauser for Dave's birthday present. Evander said he didn't want to sell it.

Toots said, "Who said anything about selling it?" and smiled suggestively. Evander hastily replied, "I'll take four hundred dollars for it." Toots gave him the money.

The next year when Dave came to Camp Perry for the National Matches, Evander fully expected for Toots to come along. The three of them had discussed it on his visit the previous fall. Instead Dave came alone and without the wedding band.

Evander didn't ask him about it. He waited. On the second night, Evander asked Dave if he would like to go to the Mona Mi with him for dinner. The Mona Mi was a restaurant and winery that was one of the nicer places to eat in the area. Dave took him up and halfway through the second glass of Riesling, the story began...

"When she moved in, she had this little ivory box that she sat on the dresser. She told me that it was private and that I should never look in the box. I agreed as everyone has something they don't want to share. I never touched it." Dave told the story, looking miserable.

"This spring, a wood duck came down the chimney, it's happened before in the spring. They're looking for a place to nest and the chimney looks good to them. The duck got into the house and knocked a few things over by the time I came home. Toots was not at home at the time. I got a towel and chased the bird into the bedroom where I shut the door and figured I'd throw the towel over her and get her out of the house. The duck knocked the ivory box off the dresser and broke it. I caught her and let her out." He sat there swirling the wine in his glass, his eyes welling up in tears.

Evander waited for him to gain his composure, his mind going through all the things that might have been in the box. He imagined letters from a lost lover, some horrible secret from her childhood, it could have been anything.

Dave looked at him, knowing what Evander was waiting to hear. He took a deep breath and said, "eight hundred dollars and four perfect Royal Coachman flies." Dave finished off the half glass of wine and sat back.

Evander was even more puzzled than before. His mind raced; had he missed part of the story? "I don't get it," he said.

"When she got home she explained that she had not been faithful to me during our marriage and that when she had cheated on me, she had tied a fly and put it in the box. My thoughts were that we had been married for almost two years and that there was hope. Then I asked her what the eight hundred dollars was for." Dave's face turned red, the vein in his forehead bulged and he burst into tears and hid his face in his hands.

Evander sat there stunned. What had happend

that had turned this tough man into Jello? He didn't want to ask but he had to. Finally he asked, "What was the money for?"

Dave wiped his face with his napkin, composed himself, filled his wine glass and topped off Evander's. He said "Every time she got a dozen, she sold'em."

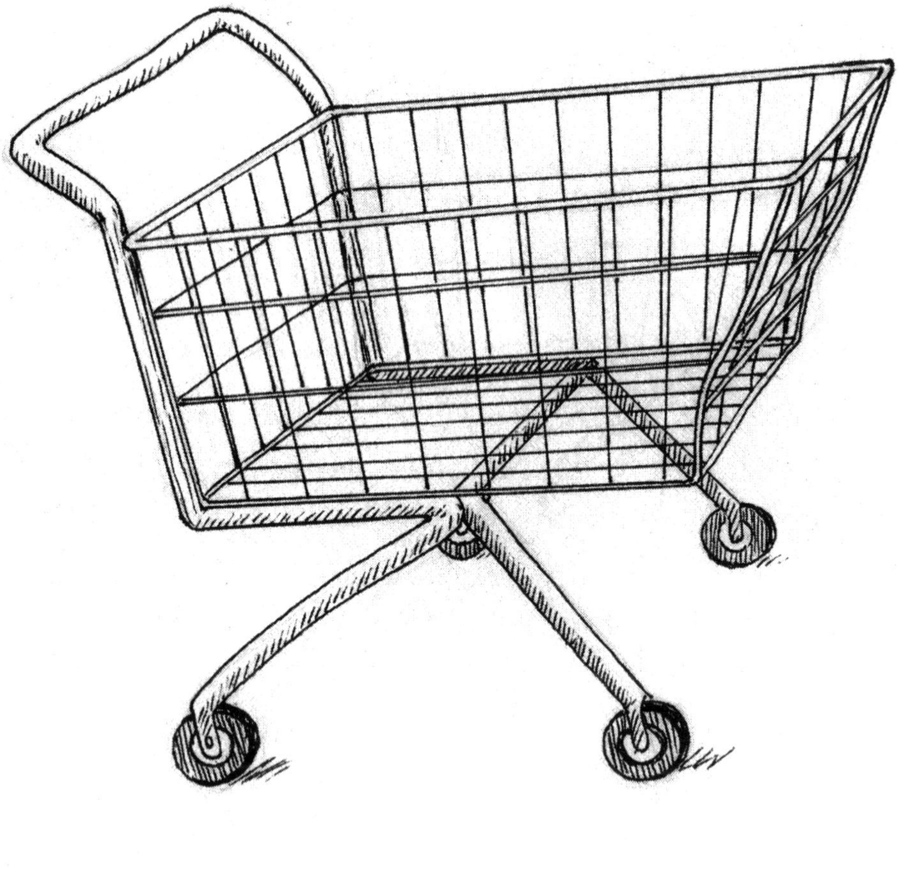

Eddy, Evander and the Big Fish

Uncle Evander was never a fan of pier fishing. In salt water, he was a surf fisherman, or he fished from a boat. He was not into trolling; he would do it for really big fish though, provided it was the only way. He liked to catch big fish. He could enjoy catching small fish if that was all there was or if the action was hot, but the big fish always got his attention.

Every year, in the fall, my family went to Kure Beach or Carolina Beach for the full moon of October. We fished a lot on the piers. There were four of them at the time. One was the old Kure Beach Pier that Robert Ruark wrote about. It was in downtown Kure Beach and was almost the biggest thing in the town. It never felt very personal to me; of course, I was young when Mama and Daddy fished there, so maybe that had something to do with it.

The next pier north was the Center Pier; I have no recollection of it at all. My Uncle Bill fished there, but I don't think Daddy ever did. I think there was too much drinking there. Then there was the Steel Pier. I think that that one has been gone a long time. Steel is a good thing, but salt water is bound to have its way sooner or later. Our pier was the Carolina Beach, or North Pier, as we called it. It was home.

The tackle shop at the Carolina Beach Pier didn't block the entrance to the pier. It was like the owners there trusted you more than the other piers. You could walk up onto the pier without going in at all. Not that anyone who fished would even consider going out on the pier without checking out the tackle shop. They had more hardcore fishing stuff than the other piers. There were no pinball or baseball machines at the North Pier. They didn't sell beach souvenirs either; they were about fishing. They had a big display case on the right as you came in the door with every kind of reel you could want. There was a bait counter there, too. You could get shrimp, mullet, bloodworms, and sometimes they would have exotic baits such as little frozen finger mullet.

On the ceiling hung all the big fishing rods for surf fishing, Penn Nines mostly mounted on fiberglass rods with a few old Calcutta bamboo rods left over. As I was growing up there was a new style of reel showing up, the spinning reel. The display case was filled with Quicks and Mitchells in several sizes. To the left there were coolers, lard cans, nets, and cases of beer and soft drinks waiting to be put into the coolers.

The bathrooms were over in the left rear corner. Straight in front of you when you came in the door was the lunch counter. It had stools in front of it and a plywood top with about a half-inch of varnish and an aluminum band on the edge. There was a sign over the counter that gave the prices for hotdogs, hamburgers, grilled cheese sandwiches, french fries, onion rings, and other such fare. You could even get your fish that you caught cooked and served with all the fixings; I don't remember what that cost, but for some reason I wish I did.

What really made the North Pier seem like home, though, was Grandma. She wasn't my grandma, I don't know if she was really anybody's grandma. She was Grandma to us. Daddy had always called her Grandma; even before she and Sam, her husband, got the pier. She'd run a little bait shop close to the harbor where the charter boats were moored up when Daddy first met her. Daddy bought bait from her for a couple of years before she and Sam got the pier. She was probably not much older than Daddy, but she had straight grey hair, and she pulled it back in a bun. She looked like a grandma.

She had the nature of a grandma, too. She always had time to talk to kids and even took me shelling on her day off once. She had a nature of extreme wisdom and worldliness to me. I once watched with amazement when a man came in the tackle shop for breakfast. He'd fished all night, he said. He ordered a bowl of cornflakes with beer on them. Grandma never even flinched. She poured the cornflakes into the bowl, opened the beer with the hinged can opener they used in those days (I haven't seen one of those in a long time), and poured the beer over the corn flakes. He sat at the bar and ate them just like he did it every day. I looked at them and was amazed that they looked just like regular corn flakes since the beer had foamed up and was white on top. When he left, I told Grandma I had never heard of that before. She smiled and said she hadn't either. You couldn't tell it by the way she handled it, though.

Grandma's husband was Sam Blake, a short, tough, little man who reminded me of Popeye. He smoked a pipe, had gnarled weathered hands, and inhaled through his mouth and exhaled through his nose when he was working on something tedious. I considered him a mechanical genius because he could take a Penn Nine completely apart, fix it, and put it back together again. He'd spent some time as a commercial fisherman, and I could listen to him talk for hours.

But this story's about something else. Uncle Evander had come down to the beach while we were having our annual week's trip, and he had brought Eddy Campbell with him.

Actually, Eddy had brought Uncle Evander. My illustrious uncle hated to drive. He'd make up all sorts of excuses to keep from having to drive. He'd have a bad tire or perhaps his radiator had been leaking. He always came up with an excuse. A lot of his friends noticed it and didn't mind too much. After all, if he got started telling a story or something like that, he'd run past an exit and then just wheel around and head back, and Evander told a lot of stories. He was really pretty safe. He could just be kind of un-nerving. I really think Eddy didn't mind driving; he just needed something to harp about.

Eddy had a nice truck, and he resented Evander's constantly dropping wrappers and other stuff onto the floor of his truck. Evander rarely offered to pay for gas, either. Instead, he'd wait till they'd stopped at a cheap restaurant and offer to pay for Eddy's dinner. This normally happened if Eddy had ordered the cheapest thing on the menu. Evander's cigars were another issue. He would ask

Eddy, Evander and the Big Fish

Eddy if he could smoke, and Eddy felt guilty not letting him.

Still, all things considered, they really had a great relationship. They hadn't known each other all that long. But they'd hit it off right from the start. Eddy had been in the Marines, and he always looked like a Marine. He was short and athletic looking, he had a short haircut, he dressed neat, and he wore small glasses that made him look like a bookworm who could handle himself in a fight.

On the day of their departure for the beach, Eddy came by to pick Evander up at 4:30 a.m. Evander had not been quite ready and had loaded Eddy's truck with a ton of things he had brought along. He'd smoked a cigar as soon as they were on the highway and then gone to sleep. At about 8:00 they were on the long stretch of straight highway just past the town of Dunn. Eddy came up behind a large tow truck towing a semi tractor backwards. He started to pass it, and then he fell back behind it and considered his idea.

He appreciated Evander; it wasn't that he didn't. He just resented the way that my uncle sometimes took advantage of him. The problem with being mad at Evander, and plenty of people tried, was that he was occasionally so generous that you felt guilty. When I was twelve, he asked me one day why I wasn't squirrel hunting. I had told him that I didn't have the money to buy .22 ammunition and that I only had a few. I was going to go hunting with my buddy, Rayvon, on Saturday, and I had to save my ammunition. He went out to his little VW camper he owned at the time and came back with a whole brick of Super X Winchester, my preferred brand.

I asked him why he gave me a whole brick instead of just a box, and he replied "I tend to be self centered and thoughtless sometimes; if I do really nice things for you when I'm not, you'll find it easy to forgive me when I am." That kind of summed up my uncle when he was younger, periods of selfishness interspersed with acts of unreasonable kindness and generosity. As I grew up, in retrospect, it seems he did, too, becoming more generous and thoughtful as he aged.

That was what made it hard for Eddy to follow up with his idea. He really loved Evander, he just got irritated with him. He decided after he thought about it a while, that since his plan would be one that Evander could appreciate, he should do it. Evander loved excitement more than anyone, and Eddy knew this. He also considered that Evander would enjoy it later when he told the story, and so, he proceeded.

He began to move closer to the semi tractor, so close that you could see the individual bugs on the grill. It was a Mack tractor. It was bright red and huge. They were only a few feet from the front bumper. He laid on the horn and screamed at the top of his lungs....

Uncle Evander awoke with a start; his eyes opened and all he could see was the front of the tractor. He screamed too, and vibrated, as he compressed himself into the seat back. He drew his arms up to his chest and gasped unintelligible noises. For a second, he thought he'd somehow slowed time down and that it was going to start back up at any second. Then the realization came to him what had happened. The color came back to his face, he began to breathe again and he slowly turned to look at Eddy. Eddy could see that there were tears in his eyes. A smile grew across his face. "That was one of the best tricks I've ever seen; stop up here at the diner on the right and I'll buy your breakfast."

We were staying in Harvey Binswinger's beach house and there was plenty of room. When Eddy and Evander arrived, they stayed in the room with me as it had two sets of bunk beds. Before they could unload the car, Evander had to tell everybody what Eddy had done to him, and as he told it, they laughed until tears came to their eyes.

Uncle Evander had more fishing tackle than anyone I ever knew. It was good stuff, too. He would get a new rod every time he found one that was better than the one he had. This was really good because I sometimes got his rejects, which were better than anything my family had. He had all categories of tackle. He had big Hatteras Heaver surf rods with exotic Ambassador reels, he had heavy trolling gear with big gold Fin Nor reels that cost more than some people's cars, and he had delicate little fly rods made of bamboo that he sometimes called buggy whips. For this trip he'd brought several rods that were suited to the kind of fishing we did: light surf rods that would throw four ounces of sinker and some smaller stuff for plugging blues and speckled trout.

Eddy had lots of tackle too, though not as much, and it wasn't like Evander's. Eddy's rods came from hardware stores, not expensive catalogs. They were kind of unkempt. Some of the reels were rusty, the guides on the rods were corroded, and the reels sometimes sounded like they needed oil.

Once they'd unpacked, they decided to walk out on the pier and see what the water looked like. I tagged along. Eddy would have been happy to just fish on the pier, like the majority of people, but Evander had ideas of going down to Fort Fisher and trying to catch a puppy drum below the rocks, an unusual formation of boulders that extended out into the ocean. Once on the pier though, they had a change of plans. As they walked out to the end, they saw a huge commotion and a big crowd had gathered. They got there just as a 25 pound king mackerel came over the rail in the pipe frame net that was used when someone caught something big on the pier. Another fish had been landed about an hour ago, the crowd told them.

They made their plans and set to work right away. Uncle Evander gave me five dollars and told me to go to the tackle shop and get three pier tickets, a pound of shrimp, and two pounds of mullet. They went to get the rods. When I got back, they were arguing about the rods and how Eddy should take better care of his stuff. We baited up with Fireball rigs to try to catch some bluefish for bait. Evander let me use one of his Mitchell 300s and I was in love. I'd never had a rod this good in my hands before, and the mystery of why he spent so much money on tackle was solved. I resolved to have tackle like that when I grew up. I would not be happy with my fishing equipment for a long time after that day.

Once we caught the first blue, they left me to revel in my uncle's prestigious tackle while they rigged and baited up the mackerel rods. I was about fifty feet from the end of the pier, and they were on the end. I heard more heated discussion about Eddy's lack of maintenance. It seemed that one of the reel's drags was locked up. Evander was upset that he hadn't brought bigger tackle and complained that they wouldn't have this problem if Eddy took better care of his stuff.

The argument was conducted against the background noise of a tiny brown Chihuahua dog that yapped continually. Eddy argued that that the stuck drag didn't make any difference since they were going to use that rod as an anchor rod, and finally Evander quit raving. They put a heavy twelve ounce sinker on the line of the reel with the stuck drag, and Eddy cast it out as far as he could. They then put the little ten-inch bluefish on a big hook with a float on the other rod and attached this rig to the anchor line with a sort of clothespin. "When the big fish hits, he'll take the line from the anchor rod and we'll bring it in and play the fish on the other rod," they explained. I thought they were very smart.

They settled down to fish, and even the little yappy dog got quiet. They'd been set up about twenty minutes when I heard the clicker on the big reel scream. They were shouting in excitement. "I think it's a shark," Eddy said, "but it's a big one."

"It could be a really large drum," Uncle Evander murmured. He was always optimistic.

Whatever it was, it was strong. It was pulling line out, and while Eddy held the fighting rod, Evander brought in the anchor rod to prevent fouling. The spool on the fighting rod got pretty small, and as it got smaller the crowd on the end of the pier got bigger. Everyone was speculating on what it was, and the little dog started yapping again. The line on the reel was starting to get dangerously small; you could see the spool at one point. But Eddy started to pump it up and wind it down and get some line back.

Just as he was getting a comfortable margin,

disaster struck. The gears in the fighting reel started making grinding noises. Then sometimes they would jerk when Eddy put too much pressure on them. Then they locked up completely.

It was almost a riot on the end of that pier. The onlookers were making stupid suggestions. Evander was about to blow a cap, and Eddy was stressed beyond belief. The little dog was yapping like mad. Maybe it was a shark, but they wanted to get it in. Then the fish quit going out. You could see the line swing north, he was just changing direction. Uncle Evander had an idea; he pulled off even more line from the reel and tied it to an old A&P shopping buggy that just happened to be on the pier. "Eddy, you hold the rod and fight the fish, and I'll control the line. "Dick," he told me, "go to the tackle shop and have Sam bring a big rod and reel for us to tie onto."

Even I understood the plan. Now I really thought he was smart. I ran as hard as I could and burst into the tackle shop out of breath. It probably took two minutes to get Sam to understand what we needed, but once he did, he grabbed a big rod and ran as fast as his short legs could carry him out to the end of the pier. He was faster than me.

Sam burst through the crowd like a bull goes through broom sage, and as I approached the backside of the crowd, I knew something had gone wrong. It was silent as an empty church. Eddy and Evander were looking forlornly over the rail, and Sam was quietly saying, "He must have gone nuts. I never saw anything like that."

I asked a man who was holding a hotdog and had mustard on his lip what had happened. "It was going pretty well" he said while chewing. "They were

Eddy, Evander and the Big Fish

working the fish and gaining some. Then the fish made a strong run and the handle of the shopping cart broke off in your uncle's hands. Eddy saw it coming and dodged the cart. It went over the rail, but that little dog must have gone crazy. He chased the cart down the pier, and when it went over the rail, he jumped over the rail in hot pursuit. He just dove in and never came up." It was quiet again.

Then I became aware of someone shouting "Jojo! Jojo!" It was a really big man in black swim trunks, a Hawaiian shirt, and a straw hat. "Has anyone seen my dog?" he asked.

The man with a hotdog and mustard on his lip answered, "Your dog went crazy and jumped over the rail into the water."

Wiping the sweat off his face with the Hawaiian shirt the big man said, "That couldn't have been my dog, I had him tied to an A&P buggy."

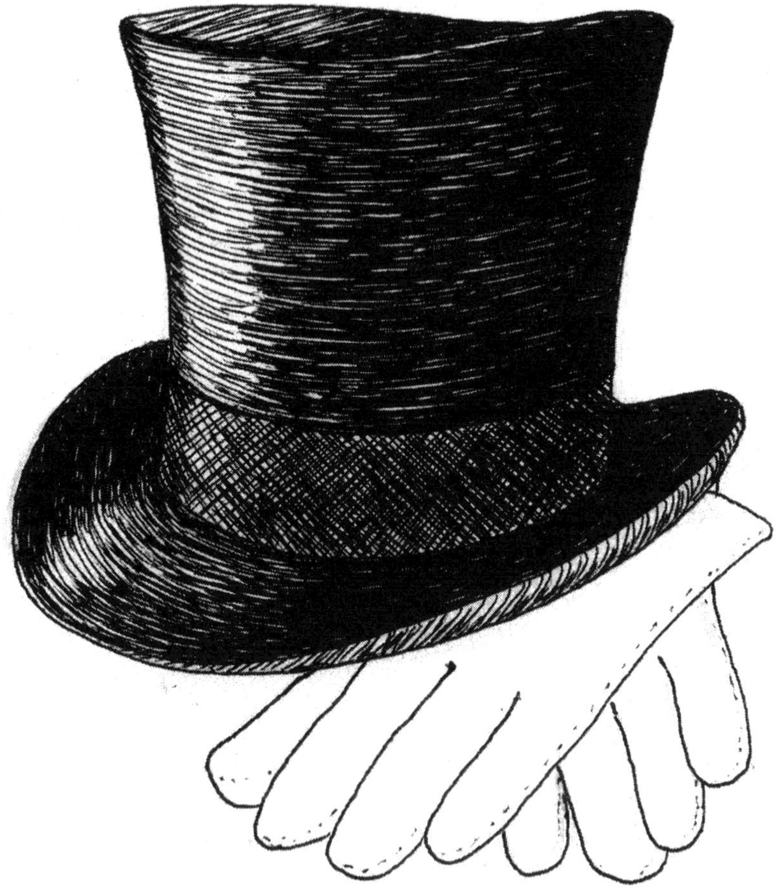

Why Uncle Evander Left New Orleans

Uncle Evander liked New Orleans. He loved the food, he loved the music, and it was his idea of what a city should be. Well, the Quarter was, anyway. He didn't have much to do with the areas outside the Quarter. His little Rampart Street Hotel was right on the north edge of the Quarter. He was making a pretty good living, too.

The restaurant had a good local following, and he had a lot of friends around the Quarter who recommended them to out-of-towners. His partner in the business, Bill Lagle, was a true friend and there were never squabbles in that area. The worst problem they had was keeping someone who could handle the place when they ran down to Venice for some fishing or to their hunting camp in Grand Isle. Louisiana truly was a sportsman's paradise in those days.

My uncle didn't care that much for deer hunting. He liked waterfowling, he loved to shoot doves, and he liked to quail hunt. He liked to fish, and there was nothing that made him happier than to tangle with a big redfish with a nice casting rod and one of his newfangled Ambassador reels.

My folks didn't understand the kind of life Uncle Evander lived and where he lived it, but then, they were straight-laced people who were pretty conservative. They just saw him as someone who never grew up, and truly, in a lot of ways, he never did. Uncle Evander was conservative though; It's just that, in relation to them, he was a wild one. His conservatism cost him in the Quarter, too. It was a pretty liberal place even back then.

A lot of the people who were there just didn't fit anywhere else. People like that tend to be angry at the rest of society because they feel it treated them unfairly. Many of his friends had radical ideas and wanted to change the way society worked. Very often, their interest was to make it work better for them. Uncle Evander didn't argue with them; he just had his own opinions. He was conservative, but not a conservative as it's described today. His brand of conservatism was that, if something worked, it didn't need fixing. He recognized a lot of things that needed fixing.

Everybody liked him because they knew he really cared for them. Some of his friends would have ridden him out of town on a rail if they'd have known his real position on some issues near to their hearts. He was not afraid to express his views; he was just too polite to argue.

He was just the kind of guy that people like and he liked almost everybody. His friends were a diverse group — from business people, doctors and lawyers, to musicians and even bums and hustlers. New Orleans had plenty of them in those days. He would meet a stranger on the street and talk for half an hour. He enjoyed talking to the bums as much as the doctors. Often, the bums would wind up getting a big bowl of gumbo and a French roll on the back steps of the kitchen. The doctors would eat in the dining room and pay full price.

When someone brought a friend in who'd never met Evander before, they'd always have to tell a story about something he'd done that was funny. He was famous for his stories and exaggerations. He used to say there was no sense in telling a dull story when it was just as easy to tell an exciting one.

There were two brothers in the Quarter who worked as roofers: David and Bill Spivey. David was a handsome, charming man who was adored by his brother as well as most of the girls they knew. One day Uncle Evander passed Bill on the street, and he said, "Tell me a big lie, Evander."

My uncle never slowed down as he said, " I don't have time for that stuff now; David just fell off the roof of the Café du Monde!" Uncle Evander walked fast down Toulouse and turned up Decatur with Bill in hot pursuit. When he got to the café, he just walked in and started talking to Jack Robichaux about his last trip to Grand Isle. David was up on the roof spreading tar, totally uninjured.

About a minute later, Bill came in, red-faced and mad as a bull. "David didn't fall off the roof. I came all the way down here for nothing!" he bellowed.

Uncle Evander was calm and never cracked a smile as he said, "You told me to tell you a big lie."

There was a rough element to the Quarter even in those days, and my uncle could handle himself when he had to, but that didn't happen much. The Rampart Street Hotel was never robbed, but there were a few altercations over the years as the rooms were often rented by women who had less than stellar reputations. Crime does happen though, and he always had a 12 gauge Fox shotgun lying on a towel under the old brass National cash register in the grill. He had a lot of other guns, but that was the one he used for about just everything. He could shoot it, too.

There were a lot of diversions in the Quarter. My uncle loved music, and you could find it everywhere. He had a lot of friends who played, and he played a little himself. He had learned to play listening to Harmonica Frank Floyd and picked up a little guitar as well. Sometimes on Sunday afternoons a group of friends would gather in the lobby of the hotel and play their songs. Some were solos, some were a couple of musicians together, and sometimes everybody joined in. Most of the time, when someone played a gospel song, everybody joined in.

One of the guys who came on Sunday afternoons was Bobby Bean, who played out on the docks every morning for tips. Sometimes Evander would go buy a Danish and a coffee at Kaldi's Coffee House, carry it across the railroad tracks, and sit and listen to him. Bobby played a saxophone like a seagull plays the wind, and he just kind of made it murmur the tune. The music would just rise and fall and roll and flow out of that saxophone, and my uncle would lean back on those rough boards with a fat cigar between his fingers and his straw hat almost down over his eyes, and look as peaceful as a sleeping bird dog. I think he was the happiest I ever saw him when he was sitting out there on the pine bench next to the biggest river in North America.

Bobby was one of the best sax players my

Why Uncle Evander Left New Orleans

uncle knew, and one day when I was with him, he asked Bobby why he didn't play in a band. Bobby said that he liked to play and he made enough money to live off of in tips on the quay. "If I played in a band it would turn into work. I don't have to work the way it is now," he shrugged.

As we crossed the railroad tracks heading back into the Quarter, Evander said, "Dick, Bobby isn't just a great saxophone player; he's a smart man."

One of the most flamboyant entertainers in the Quarter, however, was Warpo the Magnificent. Warpo wore outlandish clothes for the times. I saw pictures of him many years later and I assumed him to be the original hippie. He had long hair, and sometimes he braided it. He wore a little pistol on a chain around his neck, and I think it was real. He sold magic tricks and did shows in some of the bars. He was sure that he could make the big time if he could just get the right exposure.

Evander liked Warpo and felt he had real talent as a magician. He fished with Robert Michaux, who ran the big opera house on the corner of Bourbon and Toulouse, and talked with him about letting Warpo put together a magic show in the opera house. Robert thought Warpo just wasn't up for big time yet. One Wednesday, Evander invited Robert to go fishing with him out of Venice, Louisiana and also invited Warpo. Spending a day with Warpo convinced Robert that, maybe, Warpo could handle a big show, and on the ride home, Evander and Warpo finally persuaded Robert to give him a gig in the big venue. Warpo promised to work every day for weeks preceding the event on his routine in total secrecy, and he swore it was going to be the best show he had ever done, by far.

Warpo knew almost everyone in the Quarter; it was a small community, when you took the visitors out. This meant rumors spread quickly. Warpo raised some curiosity about the nature of his show when he started getting his props together. He approached David and Bill Spivey about borrowing their scaffold equipment, and he said he needed twenty-eight feet. That would be enough to get to the ceiling of the Opera House.

He talked to Madam Dianne, who ran the voodoo shop, about using some of her cats in the show. He told her that he needed twenty cats and promised that they would not be harmed.

He negotiated with Freddie Thibodaux to borrow Joe, the big black horse that pulled Freddie's carriage. He borrowed money from Jimmy, at Kaldi's Coffee house, to purchase a Homelite sixteen-inch chain saw.

People talked of strange smells coming from his apartment over the Olde Absinth Bar, on Crazy Corner. He was certainly generating some excitement. Warpo was a changed man. He had energy and enthusiasm. Just the fact that he had a big show coming up increased his sales on the street by fifty percent.

Warpo's stock in the Quarter was on the upswing, but fate would cause my uncle's stock to fall. It was just one of those things brought about by fate that no one ever understands. Sometimes a man does the right thing for another man and it just doesn't turn out the way it's expected.

Almost everyone in the Quarter planned to go to Warpo's grand debut into the big time. There were arguments about who was going to work in

Why Uncle Evander Left New Orleans

the strip clubs because all the girls wanted to attend the show. Several of the souvenir shops, on Bourbon Street, planned to close during the show and open back up just after to take advantage of all the traffic the event would cause.

The Quarter was in a fever pitch due to the rumors and curiosity about what Warpo was going to do. Betty Sue Crosby, a pretty but portly girl who worked in the ice plant, was rumored to be part of the show, but refused to tell anything though she was constantly questioned. There were even rumors that Warpo had hypnotized her and that she truly had no memory of their practices. The price of tickets in private hands soared, as all tickets were sold out two weeks before the show.

The night of the big show, Uncle Evander was there early. He was amazed at the crowd. Robert was beside himself with pleasure. He filled the opera house on a regular basis, but this was different. A local boy, if you could call anyone in the Quarter local, was going to make it big based on his generosity. Giving Warpo a chance at the big time made Robert a celebrity, even though nothing had happened yet.

The crowd represented the whole social structure of the Quarter. The prominent members of the local citizenry were seated in the front rows and tables just in front of the stage. The back rows up in the cheap seats were full of panhandlers, rough girls, shop workers, waitresses, cooks and tradesmen. My uncle sat pretty close to the front as his connections had assured him a reasonably good seat.

The show began with a bang. When Warpo came out on the stage, there were gasps from everyone who knew him. His hair was clipped short and impeccably styled; he was dressed in tails and a top hat; the beard and disheveled mustache were gone and he had the look of a polished performer. When he spoke, his normally weedy voice thundered through the hall. "Ladies and Gentlemen, would you kindly welcome my assistant." This reedy voiced street magician suddenly displayed all the polish of a TV spokesman.

When Betty Sue came out, the crowd went into a hushed attitude of amazement. She was dressed in a tiny costume, racy even for New Orleans, and she was slender in the parts of her anatomy where slender is desirable and magnificent in the areas where it is not. As Betty Sue paraded around the stage, Warpo boomed, "Ta-Daa!" in his new stage voice. This had a profound, inside meaning for those who knew him since that was the way he ended each trick he completed at his flimsy card table, in the French Market.

Warpo exhibited complete control of the crowd. They were stunned and amazed even before he began the first act. There was a blast from a silver whistle around his neck and twenty of Madame Dianne's housecats came out on the stage wearing feathered plumes from their shoulders. They trotted single file in perfect cadence out onto the stage and continued to trot in a circle. "Ta-Daa!" roared Warpo.

The new exciting Warpo then made a speech announcing that he was grateful for this opportunity to entertain and amaze them and that this would be a night they would remember for the rest of their lives. He was right.

Just as he was finishing up, Joe, the carriage

horse, came out onto the stage and trotted his way into the formation of cantering housecats. The housecats began to weave in formation between Joe's huge trotting feet as Warpo arranged a series of round platforms of increasing height along the back side of the living circle formed by the twenty cantering housecats and the huge carriage horse.

He blew the whistle and, on each revolution of the spectacle, one housecat peeled away from the formation and leaped from one platform to the next until he was high enough to leap onto Joe's broad back. This continued until all the cats were riding on the horse's back, the fancy ribbons and feathers on their shoulders flowing in the breeze. "Ta-Daa!" roared Warpo, dropping to one knee, and the mesmerized crowd finally came to their senses enough to give him a wild round of applause. Men were slapping each other on the back and women were crying.

Betty Sue produced a small doctor's bag and Warpo held it up to the audience. Her polished movements and intoxicating torso fascinated the excited (and at the same time disbelieving) audience. Warpo blew the whistle again, and on each revolution of the procession of cats and horse, a cat would jump into the tiny doctor bag. This continued until the cats had all disappeared into the tiny bag. "Ta-Daa!!" roared Warpo and the crowd went wild.

Warpo then approached the front and center seats of the theatre, and opening the small bag, he shook the contents out. About a dozen white doves flew out and circled the stage. "Ta-Daa!!" roared Warpo. As this happened, people in the crowd began to notice Madam Dianne's cats wandering around among the seats. Some had feathers in their mouths. This time the crowd was silent except for hushed murmurings about how Warpo was destined for certain fame.

Next, Betty Sue came out on stage with a fishing rod that had a sparkling lure on the line. He made a cast out into the crowd, but the lure never fell into the crowd. Instead it flashed a brilliant light, and a large live redfish appeared on the line suspended above the crowd. The fish struggled and made runs, back and forth over the crowd's heads as if they were on the bottom of the river witnessing the scene. Warpo landed the fish, dropped him on the stage, and made another cast. A brilliant flash of light and another larger fish appeared struggling against the straining line. He continued until the stage was covered with wet, flopping redfish. Betty Sue took the rod, and Warpo raised his arms, dropped to one knee, and in his booming voice roared, "TA-DAA!!"

He blew the whistle, and the cats converged on the stage and began dragging the fish off the stage, the larger fish requiring two cats to drag them all off. He then motioned for silence. Warpo then announced he needed a volunteer from the audience, and this was where my uncle's troubles began. Uncle Evander would volunteer for anything. He had a spirit of adventure I have never seen equaled, and this time was no exception. His hand was up before anyone else could contemplate the proposition.

Once acknowledged, he swaggered up to the stage just like he was going to pick up a trophy, and in an instant, he was at Warpo's side.

Warpo announced that this was a very dangerous trick and should not be tried at home.

Why Uncle Evander Left New Orleans

Betty Sue danced in holding a two-pound hammer and handed it to Warpo. With a flourish Warpo handed it to Uncle Evander, and using his new announcer voice, he told my uncle that he was to hit him as hard as he could on the temple once Warpo had placed his head on the tallest of the platforms the cats had used.

He laid his head on the platform. The crowd was as silent as a windless, snowy night in the Arctic. "Ready!" he roared in the new and exciting voice. "OK!" he said, a little quieter than he had been. Uncle Evander swung the hammer, but he didn't hit as hard as he could. He hit about as hard as you would if you were going to make a good lick on a nail that was already started. He later told me he just couldn't hit Warpo that hard even though he had faith in Warpo's magic tricks after what he had just witnessed.

When the hammer blow fell, Warpo just slumped onto the floor and lay motionless. The crowd was motionless, too. You could hear the breathing of the people next to you. My uncle just stood there. Ten seconds passed, then twenty. At about a minute, Uncle Evander noticed a tiny drop of blood coming from Warpo's ear and decided that the trick had gone wrong. "Ladies and Gentlemen," his voice sounded thin and weak after Warpo's booming announcements, "I believe something has gone wrong."

The doctors said Warpo had a fractured skull and a concussion and that he might not survive. Uncle Evander was miserable. In the first place, he really liked Warpo; they'd been friends for several years. He felt guilty even though he'd done exactly as instructed, except he hadn't hit as hard as he could.

The worst thing was the way other people treated and looked at him. They'd been so excited at what was going to happen to Warpo after the word got out about this incredible show. They were going to see one of the regular, or even less than regular, make it big. It was like seeing someone close to you win the lottery. You weren't any better off, but you got a boost just from the proximity. Now the miracle boy was in the hospital and probably wouldn't make it.

On top of that, nobody would ever know how Warpo had done all the tricks. Nor would they ever know what else he had in store. Betty Sue swore she didn't remember any of the rehearsals, though her weight loss and physical attributes stayed with her after the performance.

There was no way that you could blame Evander on a logical basis, but there aren't a lot of logical people in the French Quarter, of New Orleans; in fact, I guess there aren't a lot of logical people anywhere. People there are passionate, most operate on feelings, and Evander got the feeling that he was not as popular as he had been. In fact, he got the feeling of outright resentment.

The only one who'd benefited from the whole thing was Betty Sue. She was no longer the pretty, but portly girl who worked at the ice plant. She was now Betty Sue Crosby, the beautiful girl who'd helped Warpo in his attempt to escape mediocrity. She soon married a wealthy advertising agent and moved to New York City.

Uncle Evander felt he'd lost most of his friends in the Quarter and that he was a liability to the ones he hadn't lost. He also had concerns that, if charged with manslaughter in the event of Warpo's death, the people who were not too happy with him would be his jury.

One night, after making arrangements with Bill to buy his half of the business, Evander packed his clothes and fishing rods, his Fox shotgun and the contents of the wall safe, in the '39 Pontiac and drove out of town, headed for Key West. It was time to start over.

Epilogue

Warpo didn't die. He was in a coma for nine years and is successfully practicing magic today. One day when the nurse came into his room to change his sheets, he jumped out of the bed, went down on one knee, raised his arms, and squeaked, "Ta-Daa!"

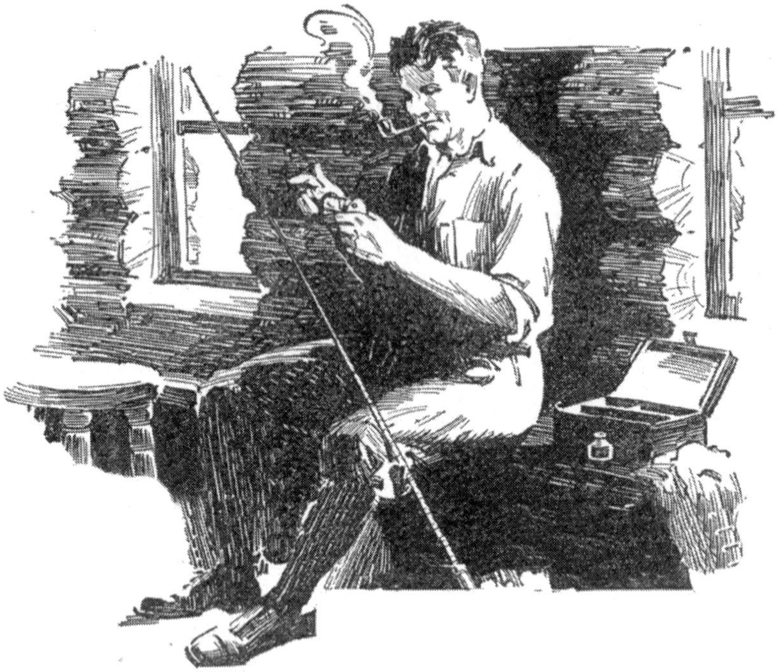

Bob and the White 40 Quart Cooler

Bob Craft loved to fish, but he was no purist. He loved to eat fish and didn't care that much for catch and release. Bob practiced filet and release. He had little interest in the shad fishing Evander and I did in the spring. Evander tried to interest him in the shad on the basis that he could catch them on a fly rod. He went on a shad trip with us, caught a lot of them and had a lot of fun, but then he found out how boney they were, and passed on the next trip. Evander told him that he could eat the roe of the shad, and his interest picked up again. Then he visited his friend Doc Coughlin who told him how much cholesterol there was in fish roe, and Bob, who could eat a half pound of extra sharp cheddar by himself, backed out on the next trip.

    I thought the shad were as much fun as the stripers, and Uncle Evander introduced me to catching them on a fly rod. We'd use a few feet of lead core line with braided monofilament for a running line and fish little streamers in different pastel colors. The shad ran deep as a rule, but once hooked, they would run out and up to the surface,

Bob and the White 40 Quart Cooler

making multiple jumps before we could get them to the boat. It was fine sport.

Bob was too enamored with frying what he caught to enjoy them, but he loved to fish for stripers and anguished over which fish to keep since you could only keep three. Of course, he'd only fish on keeper days, Saturday, Sunday, and Wednesday in those days. Once the keeper season was over, he was pretty much done with the stripers and went after crappie, a fish my uncle detested. Evander claimed that life was too short to fish for little fish, shoot ugly shotguns, and wear uncomfortable shoes. Bob loved crappie and fished for them until the warmer water of summer turned them off, and then he went after catfish.

Normally, Bob's disdain for catch and release wasn't a problem for Evander since he could always find someone interested in catching shad early and stripers once the keeper season was over. This particular year, it turned out to be a difficulty.

Evander had been in Staunton, Virginia where Bob's son, John, was working for the Virginia Alcohol Control Board. They ran into each other at the diner, and in talking about Bob, decided it would be nice for the three of them to go fishing together. John told Evander that he, Bob's other son, David, and grandson, Nathan, were planning a trip to Maryland for croakers that next week. Evander and John cooked up a plan for the boys to go to the Roanoke instead and surprise their dad. Evander would bring Bob while John, David, and Nathan would drive down together from Virginia. The big surprise would occur when Evander and Bob showed up with them all standing at the boat dock.

While they were still at the diner, they called David and Nathan and changed the plans. It was going to be great; the only problem was that the day that had been chosen was after striper season was closed. Getting Bob to the river was going to be tough since Bob wasn't all that hot for catch and release fishing. John worried that Evander wouldn't be able to get Bob to come without revealing the surprise, but Evander said "Don't worry about that, I'll take care of it."

When Evander got home, he dropped by Bob's house. Bob was putting line on a fishing reel and had crappie tackle spread all over the kitchen table. "How about going to the Roanoke with me on the ninth?" Evander asked.

"Seasons over," Bob murmured under his breath, still concentrating on getting the line on the reel without kinks. "I'm going fishing with Frank Parker at his pond on the ninth. He's been catching a ton of crappie."

Evander wiped his face from top to bottom with his open hand. Those that knew him well knew this was a trouble sign. Bob had his back turned and didn't see it. "That's not a problem. You know how I fished with that fisheries fella last month? All you have to do is put the fish you keep in a 44 quart white cooler with your name, address and social security number on it. You can keep all the fish you can get in the cooler."

Bob turned around, his eyes were wide open. "Evander Prichart! You beat all I ever saw; you could talk your way out from in front of a firing squad! Man! We can fill the freezer!"

Evander looked troubled. "We can only do one cooler. I'll let you have all the fish. My freezer is full of ducks anyway."

Bob was touched with Evander's generosity, "You're all right, Prichart. Sometimes you're a really decent guy."

The trip went great, Bob was totally surprised when the boys showed up at the boat landing. It was good weather, and the fish bit pretty good. They caught fish early on topwaters and then went with jigs. When the fishing slowed, they switched over to live bait and drifted down the river talking about old times while taking turns on the fly rod, picking up the occasional fish. Nathan caught the biggest fish of the day, a seven pounder. It was a perfect day of fishing and friendship with some family reunion mixed in.

Everyone released their fish except Bob, who filled his cooler. By the end of the day, they'd caught stripers on jigs, flies, topwaters, and bait. Bob fished live bait more than the others and kept talking about how Evander was such a great friend to let him keep the fish.

The boys all went home with Bob to High Point to spend the next day, and an impromptu fish fry was planned for Sunday afternoon. Frank and Aileen Parker were invited since Bob had canceled with Frank and Evander had let Frank in on the surprise so he would know why.

After everyone was stuffed with Evander's fried striper filets, jalapeño potato salad, corn on the cob and cornfield green beans, Frank asked, "Bob, did you say you caught these fish yesterday? I thought the season was closed."

Bob smiled and said, "Evander pulled some strings with someone at the Marine Fisheries Department so I could keep them legally."

Bob and the White 40 Quart Cooler

Evander chuckled a little and said, "Bob, that's not exactly right. I said you could keep the fish, I never said it was legal. I just mentioned the fisheries guy. If we'd been checked, you would've gotten a ticket."

Bob's face turned beet red. "You mean you just let me keep illegal fish? Why did you have me use a 44 quart, white cooler with my name, address and social security number written on it?" Bob asked, exasperated.

"Oh," Evander replied, "That was in case we got checked. I figured if all your information was on the cooler, I wouldn't get a ticket!"

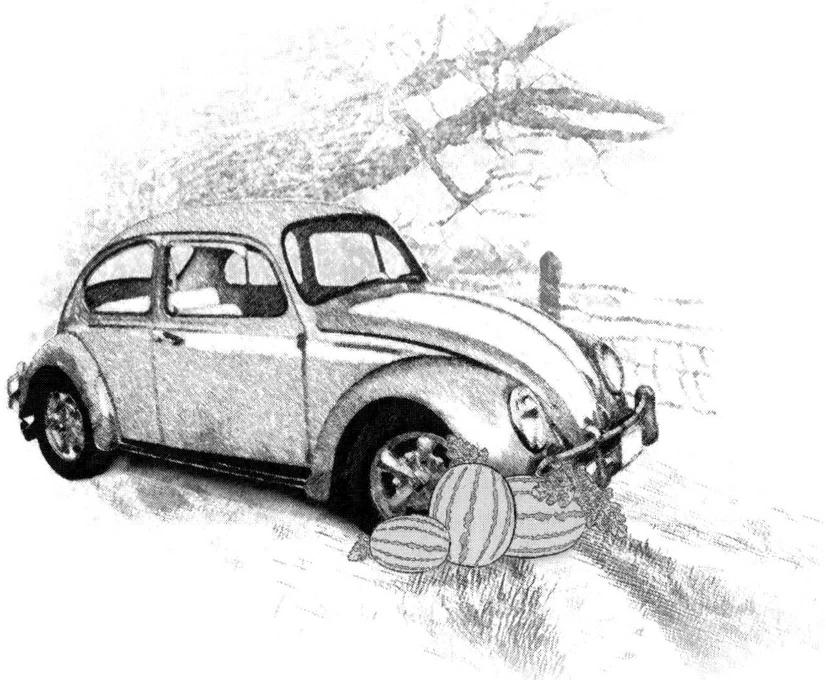

Uncle Evander Steals a Watermelon

Evander Pritchert understood human nature better than anyone I've ever known. He was also the best liar I've ever known, though he didn't believe in profiting from his lying. He saw a good lie as a work of art and, had he been an artist, he would have never sold a single painting. He believed in lying for the joy and entertainment only, as does a sidewalk artist who does beautiful chalk pictures that will be destroyed by foot traffic, or a sand sculptor who watches the waves take away his work when the tide comes in. Even as a small boy, I learned how to follow along with his games, because I knew the eventual result would be entertaining, and I could play a part, even if it was a small one.

Evander had a friend named Mike Murdoch. Mike was a bit older than Evander and sometimes he waxed romantic about adventures past. Mike had a big screened porch, and when we visited him, we always sat out on the screened porch. If the weather was cold, he built a fire in the fireplace on the porch, a feature I saw as an incredible luxury.

This particular night there was no need

for a fire; it was mid-summer and Evander and Mike were smoking cigars while sitting in those aluminum lawn chairs with the nylon webbing that everyone owned in the 50s and 60s. Mike took a big draw off his cigar and said, "I wish I could steal just one more watermelon in my life. A watermelon you raise or buy just isn't as good as one you steal."

Evander looked at me pointedly and winked. "You know, Mike, I know a guy who's a grouch and prides himself on his watermelons. I'd like nothing better than to steal one. Want to go steal one now?"

I was proud, as I always was when Evander allowed me in on a trick. It was his way of letting me know I could be trusted not to spoil a complicated scheme that might require quite a bit of effort to pull off. Mike blew out a cloud of smoke and sat forward. "Are you serious?" he asked.

"Of course I am. Let's go." Evander got up and started for the door; I got up, too, just like we stole watermelons every night. The fact was, I had never stolen a watermelon in my life, but I'd heard stories Daddy and Evander told of the adventure. Secretly, I wished we really were going to steal a watermelon, though I suspected different.

At the time, Evander owned a little white Volkswagen Bug. In the South, we called any Volkswagen a bug, the same way we called any soft drink a Coke. This little Bug would go anywhere because the engine was in the back. I learned to drive a stick shift in it, because you just let the clutch out and it took off. I climbed in the tiny back seat with Mike and Evander in front.

Mike knew Daddy, and where we lived, but he didn't know much else about the neighborhood.

Uncle Evander Steals a Watermelon

Evander took us in from the opposite direction we'd normally take, even taking a couple of dirt roads for good measure. All the way, Mike expressed doubt that we were really going to steal a watermelon, but he didn't want to back down just in case Evander was serious. When we got to Brian Criddlebaugh's tobacco barn road, I figured out the trick. Daddy owned land on both sides of Lewis Creek and we were going in the back way instead of crossing the bridge. Daddy's watermelon patch was only a hundred yards from the tobacco barn road and there was a little trail that led to the watermelon patch. The Bug would negotiate it with no trouble at all.

As we started down the trail, Evander cut the lights and the Bug crawled down to the watermelon patch. He warned us to be really quiet because the old man who owned the patch often shot at people who tried to steal melons. He explained we'd avoided going by the old man's house but the patch was close to the house and the windows would be open in summer. He painted the story so well that I could imagine Daddy sitting in his recliner hearing us and coming out to investigate.

We picked a watermelon, and another for "just in case" and the Bug crawled back up the trail still running dark. Evander claimed to have seen a flashlight and we blazed out Brian's tobacco barn road like our tail was on fire.

Back on the porch, we ate the hearts out of both melons with reckless abandon. Excess is the way of robbers, I guess. Mike smiled the whole way, and by the time the last of the watermelon heart was gone, he was remembering seeing Daddy's nonexistent flashlight beam, too.

Made in the USA
Lexington, KY
26 October 2017